Listening for God's Voice

A Discipleship Guide to a Closer Walk

for Personal Devotional Use, Small Groups or
Sunday School Classes, and Sermon Preparation for Pastors and Teachers

JesusWalk® Bible Study Series

by Dr. Ralph F. Wilson
Director, Joyful Heart Renewal Ministries

Additional books, and reprint licenses are available at:
www.jesuswalk.com/books/voice.htm

Free Participant Guide handout sheets are available at:
www.jesuswalk.com/voice/voice-lesson-handouts.pdf

JesusWalk® Publications
Loomis, California

Paperback

ISBN-13: 978-0-9962025-5-8

ISBN-10: 0-9962025-5-2

Library of Congress subject headings:

    Spiritual life – Christianity.

    God (Christianity) – Will.

Suggested Classifications

      Dewey Decimal System: 234.13

      Library of Congress: BT767.3 BV4501.2

Published by JesusWalk® Publications, P.O. Box 565, Loomis, CA 95650-0565, USA.

JesusWalk is a registered trademark and Joyful Heart is a trademark of Joyful Heart Renewal Ministries.

Unless otherwise noted, all the Bible verses quoted are from the New International Version (International Bible Society, 1973, 1978), used by permission.

12/4/2017 6:27 PM

This book is dedicated to my pastor

Greg Krieger
Rock Harbor Covenant Church
Rocklin, California

whose constant prayer is,
"Give us open ears to hear Your whispers
and courageous hearts to follow Your lead."

Preface

God can get anyone's attention by shouting. For example, on the road to Damascus, a loud voice and a bright light turned his arch enemy into a disciple. But most of the time, he prefers to speak in a softer voice, one that we can miss if we're not listening carefully.

I'm not sure anyone can be a real expert on hearing God's voice, since God controls it, not we. And I've had some embarrassing gaps in both listening and obeying – some of which I'll relate to you.

Recently, however, God has put on my heart to share with you what I have learned over 50 years of actively listening for God's voice. I've found that when I seek God for what to preach and teach, I am usually able to discern his desire. I sought the Lord about the girl to marry – and even received the date of the marriage from God. God's voice has been a huge comfort and guide for me over my lifetime. I share humbly, however, realizing that I have much to learn.

Edward Burne-Jones, 'Elijah the Prophet' (1897), stained glass, St. Martin's Church, Bramton, Cumbria, England

The focus of this study is hearing God's voice in words and in promptings. When I say "hear," I don't mean to suggest that God usually speaks in an audible voice, but that we can discern him speaking in strong impressions in our mind and spirit. It is that form of the voice of God that is what we're especially exploring in this study.

Three things aren't our focus – the spiritual gifts of prophecy, the word of knowledge, and the word of wisdom. Of course, the Holy Spirit is the common denominator between these gifts and how the normal disciple might hear God's voice and promptings. But to treat these gifts of the Spirit adequately would require a completely different kind of study – and is beyond my experience.

Nor is this a comprehensive study of God's guidance – a subject all its own. God guides us in many ways – through circumstances, other people, a Bible verse that the Holy Spirit "quickens" to us. And, of course, God's voice can be a *means* of guidance. Here, we are narrowly focusing on God's voice and promptings, to try to understand them better.

The challenge is that I am seeking to teach a learned skill or art, not a body of content. This isn't a set of objective rules you can follow to get the desired result. It is subjective. Relational. Controlled by God, not by us.

Nor can I sit down with you at Starbucks to give you feedback and help you as you learn. I know that God is fully able to speak to his people directly without any assistance. However, I believe you'll learn faster and better if you learn to listen to God as part of a Christian community. So I'll be asking you to find a mentor (if you are able), plus a spiritual partner with whom you can interact as you begin to learn what God's voice and whisperings sound like. Don't try this all by yourself – you just won't get nearly as much out of it!

I'll also be asking you secure a small journal and begin a daily Quiet Time – or renew your current practice so it is more meaningful. You'll be completing a practical assignment in each lesson – and then you'll share how it's working out with your spiritual partner. In this way you can try your wings and begin to learn to fly even before you finish the study.

However, I must warn you that you face a clear spiritual danger as you begin this course. If you settle for learning *about* God's voice without seeking to know, discern, and obey *him* yourself, you will suffer great damage, for this will have the effect of "inoculating" you against catching a full-blown case of conversing with the living God. "Be doers of the word, and not hearers only, deceiving yourselves" (James 1:22). So plan to enter fully into the process; don't just read and nod your head.

I've found that this idea of hearing God's voice is amazingly attractive to us humans. I used to take my guitar and sing at convalescent homes. By far the most often requested song among the folks of a certain generation was, "In the Garden."

> "I come to the garden alone,
> While the dew is still on the roses;
> And the voice I hear, falling on my ear,
> The Son of God discloses.
>
> And He walks with me,
> And He talks with me,
> And He tells me I am His own;

And the joy we share as we tarry there,
None other has ever known."[1]

I invite you to join me on a journey of drawing closer to Jesus, to listening for and then obeying God's voice and promptings.

Dr. Ralph F. Wilson
Loomis, California
January 1, 2018

[1] Words and music: C. Austin Miles (1912).

Table of Contents

References and Abbreviations

BDAG Walter Bauer and Frederick William Danker, *A Greek-English Lexicon of the New Testament and Other Early Christian Literature*, (Third Edition; based on previous English editions by W.F. Arndt, F.W. Gingrich, and F.W. Danker; University of Chicago Press, 1957, 1979, 2000)

ESV English Standard Version (Crossway, 2001)

Holladay William L. Holladay, *A Concise Hebrew and Aramaic Lexicon of the Old Testament*, based on the Lexical work of Ludwig Koehler and Walter Baumgartner (Grand Rapids: Eerdmans / Leiden: E. J. Brill, 1988)

ISBE Geoffrey W. Bromiley (general editor), *The International Standard Bible Encyclopedia* (Eerdmans, 1979-1988; fully revised from the 1915 edition)

KJV King James Version (Authorized Version, 1611)

Metzger Bruce M. Metzger, *A Textual Commentary on the Greek New Testament* (United Bible Societies, 1971)

NASB New American Standard Bible (The Lockman Foundation, 1960-1988)

NIV New International Version (International Bible Society, 1973, 1978)

NJB New Jerusalem Bible (Darton, Longman & Todd Ltd, 1985)

NKJV New King James Version (HarperCollins, 1982)

NRSV New Revised Standard Version (Division of Christian Education of the National Council of Churches of Christ, USA, 1989)

Thayer Joseph Thayer, *Thayer's Greek-English Lexicon* (reprint of 1889 edition).

TWOT R. Laird Harris, Gleason L. Archer, Jr., and Bruce K. Waltke, (editors), *Theological Wordbook of the Old Testament*, (2 volumes, Moody Press, 1980)

Reprint Guidelines

Copying the Handouts. In some cases, small groups or Sunday school classes would like to use these notes to study this material. That's great. An appendix provides copies of handouts designed for classes and small groups. There is no charge whatsoever to print out as many copies of the handouts as you need for participants.

Free Participant Guide handout sheets are available at:

www.jesuswalk.com/voice/voice-lesson-handouts.pdf

All charts and notes are copyrighted and must bear the line:

"Copyright © 2018, Ralph F. Wilson. All rights reserved. Reprinted by permission."

You may not resell these notes to other groups or individuals outside your congregation. You may, however, charge people in your group enough to cover your copying costs.

If you copy the book (or the majority of it) for your congregation or group, you are requested to purchase a reprint license for each book. A Reprint License, $1.50 for each copy is available for purchase at

www.jesuswalk.com/books/voice.htm

Or you may send a check to:

Dr. Ralph F. Wilson
JesusWalk Publications
PO Box 565
Loomis, CA 95650, USA

The Scripture says,

"The laborer is worthy of his hire" (Luke 10:7) and "Anyone who receives instruction in the word must share all good things with his instructor." (Galatians 6:6)

However, if you are from a third world country or an area where it is difficult to transmit money, please make a small contribution instead to help the poor in your community.

Introduction to Listening for God's Voice

Before we pursue listening for God's voice, we need to confront some patterns of unbelief or fear that may be lurking within us and keeping us from the adventure of hearing God.

1. God's Interest in Our Affairs

First, there's the belief that God doesn't really care about my everyday life – or is too busy to speak to me individually. This stems from unbelief, from an inadequate understanding of God.

Throughout the New Testament we see the common theme of God's love for us. Of the many, many verses, two will suffice to make the point:

> "We love because he first loved us." (1 John 4:19)

> "God demonstrates his own love for us in this: While we were still sinners, Christ died for us." (Romans 5:8)

Yes, my friend, God loves you personally and individually, and wants to communicate with you and you with him. It's pretty amazing, but it's true.

James J. Tissot, 'Moses sees the promised Land from Afar' (1896-1900), Gouache on board, The Jewish Museum, New York.

Related to this is a concern that God is too busy to be bothered with me and my concerns. I once asked a man whose bicycle shop was failing if I could pray for his business. He said, "No, God is too busy to be concerned with something this trivial." This comes from a wrong view of God – a God that doesn't really love individually and a God who has limited time and resources. It's as if there are only so many incoming lines to God Central and we need to keep these open for real emergencies. You can see how silly this is when you realize that God is infinite and has created the universes! So don't let these fears and wrong views of God hold you back.

2. My Worthiness

Second, there is a belief that inhibits listening for God's voice: that I'm not worthy or holy enough for God to speak to me. I find myself sinning and I feel unworthy. Why would he want to talk to a sinner like me?

The truth is that God has been talking to sinners for a long time. Consider Jacob, for example. He was a schemer and conniver who cheated his brother out of his birthright and lied to his father. Yet God loved him and began to speak to him – and in so doing changed his life forever.

True, you and I are *not* worthy, even though we try to live lives that please God. We fall short. We fail. But God extends his grace to us – pure favor that is neither earned nor deserved. Confess your sins to God and seek to be right in his eyes. Do that and you will be forgiven (1 John 1:9). Just realize that compared to God's holiness, "all our righteous acts are like filthy rags" (Isaiah 64:6). At our best, we're only *relatively* pure before God. We trust in his grace and in his righteousness alone. Don't let your sense of unworthiness keep you from seeking to hear God's voice.

3. Authority and Sufficiency of Scripture

Third, there's sometimes a belief that hearing God's voice will become a new authority for us that will diminish the authority of God's written word, the Bible, and its sufficiency for Christian living.[2] The people who hold this view might have the mantra:

"Give me a verse, not a voice."

Let me put this fear to rest. God's written word has full authority. He will say nothing to you that contradicts the Bible. Indeed, the Bible is the authority by which we can test any purported word from God.

However, *to resist listening for God's voice because you now have the Bible, places you at odds with all the examples of God's interactions with humans in the New Testament.* For men and women in Bible days, hearing God's voice didn't threaten the revelation of the Scriptures. Rather, it helped them understand what God wanted to communicate to them in the moment, to help them in their day by day lives and ministries.

To resist God speaking to us today seriously undercuts the New Testament pattern that we have been given. It would mean that God's intimate communication is not for us today. God hasn't gone mute. The Acts of the Holy Spirit continue today. Praise God.

---

[2] This is the position of some "cessationists" who believe that the miraculous gifts of the Spirit ceased at the end of the apostolic era.

4. Need for Obedience

Fourth, there's often a fear that God will tell me to do something I don't want to do. He'll tell me to go to Africa where there are snakes and insects. And you know how I hate snakes!

This fear isn't really about snakes. It's about belief in God's goodness. It's about trust. It's about obedience to God. It's about discipleship. My dear friend, you need to surrender your life and your future to Christ. He knows the journey; you don't. You can trust him to lead you every step of the way.

If you can't trust him, then what does your "Christianity" really consist of anyway? We must either wallow in our unbelief and resistance to obedience, or we stand up in faith and say, "Where you lead me I will follow." That's discipleship. Scary? Yes. But that's the adventure we see lived out by the heroes of the Old and New Testaments.

5. Going Off the Deep End

Fifth, there's a fear that if we seek to hear directly from God, we'll "go off the deep end." We'll become fanatics who are out of touch with reality. Our parents and friends might disapprove of us. Hearing voices, they'll say, is a sure sign of insanity.

Who is the author of that fear? Satan, who doesn't want you to trust Jesus and follow him where he leads you.

All of us struggle at times. You may have struggled with mental health issues such as deep loss or depression. My heart goes out to you. I hope you'll find this study helpful to you.

> Of course, certain mental health issues relate to difficulty in sorting out what's real in our world and what isn't. If that is what you're struggling with, please talk about this study with both your mental health professional *and* your pastor before taking this course. It simply isn't wise to add an additional level to your struggle with discernment – in this case, spiritual discernment – until you've reached some stability in what you're currently dealing with.

It's true, however. As you go deeper with God, your non-spiritual friends *won't* understand. They may think you've "gone off the deep end." They'll think you're strange. You have to choose: Can I trust Jesus enough to follow him fully? Do I desire the approval of people more than I desire the approval of God?

I do want to assure you, however, that you'll find God can teach you to swim quite well in the "deep end" of the pool. You won't drown, you'll flourish! I hope that as you study the Scriptures you'll jump in. The water is truly fine!

Practical Assignments

Since we're trying to develop a skill of listening for God's voice, each lesson includes a practical assignment for you to put into practice in your life that week. This is not an academic study of Bible theory, but a practical study that will result in your life being changed. So, here we go. If you'd like to see all the assignments together, so you can see where we're going, go to Appendix 2. Assignments to Sensitize You to God's Voice

What follows is your first practical assignment which I'd like you to complete before you begin the first lesson!

Week 0 Assignment. Get Ready. Find A Mentor, a Spiritual Partner, and a Notebook

As you begin this series of lessons to help you discern God's voice, I want you to find a mentor – or at least a peer with whom you can share in this new lifestyle.

Listening for God's voice and promptings, and then doing what he shows you to do, is a learned skill of sorts. But it is more than that, it is an exciting way of life.

Manual skills can be learned by watching YouTube videos. But how does a new police officer become sensitized to the problems and crimes of a neighborhood? By riding along with a more experienced officer who points things out that the average person just doesn't see. In the process, the novice officer acquires trained eyes.

Though God has helped many people learn to hear and identify God's voice and promptings on their own, that is not the easiest way to learn. It is best to **find a mentor** in your church or community to whom you can go with questions that may come up. *Make sure this is someone who actually believes in and practices listening for God.* In some churches your pastor might be this person. Or it might be a spiritually mature man or woman. On some occasions, your mentor might even attend a different church. Nevertheless, diligently search out this person by prayer and by suggestions of others.

In addition to a mentor, you need to **find a spiritual partner** who can walk this journey with you. You'll learn from each other and be able to bounce ideas off of each other. When I was in college, Edson Lee was my dormmate. We went to the same church on Sunday. But during the week we learned together a great deal together about listening to and obeying God. I can remember at the end of a day, we'd get together to share about how we had seen God in action that day. One of us would always say, "God sure knows what he is doing!"

Note: In this course we share responses to discussion questions in an online forum. But I think it is best to share your experiences in hearing God's voice with your spiritual partner and mentor, who know you, *not* online. The reason is this. In any kind of cyber sharing, people can't know you in your real-life context. Helpful, honest feedback on hearing God's voice needs to take that context into consideration. For our spiritual partners we need people who can get to know us in a more rounded way than someone would be able to online.

So find a mentor if you can – and for sure find a spiritual partner, a peer who is willing to walk this portion of the journey with you. Get this person to sign up for this study with you. Then get together often, in person or on the phone, to share how you see God working.

Beyond a mentor and a spiritual partner, **you'll need a notebook or journal** in which to write down what God is showing you. It's best if your notebook has decent binding so the pages don't start falling out. I found a journal a similar size to my Bible. What I settled on was a brand called Markings, a 5" x 8" journal by C.R. Gibson (markings.com), widely available in the United States. But really, any notebook will do. Make it a point to get one for this study.

It's absolutely essential for you to **begin or renew a daily Quiet Time**, 5 to 10 minutes (or more) that you spend with God in prayer, reading Scripture, and listening. I'll talk more about that in Lesson 1, but start today!

Here's the checklist to complete so you'll be ready to begin the study. Check it off when you've completed each item.

☐ Find a mentor.

☐ Recruit a spiritual partner to study and share with.

☐ Get a notebook.

☐ Begin or Renew a daily Quiet Time.

1. Listening for God as a Biblical Pattern (Mark 1:35; John 5:19)

Briton Rivière, 'The Temptation in the Wilderness' (1898), oil on canvas, 46 x 74 in., Guildhall Art Gallery, London.

In a few Christian traditions, listening for God's voice is a core part of one's spiritual life. But in many denominations, expecting to hear God's voice is very far from the norm – even suspect. And in a few groups, hearing God's voice today runs contrary to their view of Scripture.

So as we begin, I think it's important to observe the pattern of the Bible regarding hearing God's voice. We'll begin with the example Jesus set for us, and then consider the experience of other believers.

Three passages explain for me how Jesus sought his Father's voice and received power for ministry. The first is from Mark.

Jesus Prays in a Solitary Place (Mark 1:33-39)

In its characteristic terse style, Mark's Gospel records within the span of a few verses Jesus' early ministry by the Sea of Galilee and the calling of his first disciples – Peter, James, and John. On the Sabbath, while teaching in the synagogue in Capernaum, Jesus casts out a demon. Immediately his fame spreads throughout Galilee. He heals Peter's mother-in-law, and that evening the house is mobbed by the sick and needy from the all over the region. That's where we'll pick up the text.

> "33 The whole town gathered at the door, 34 and Jesus healed many who had various diseases. He also drove out many demons, but he would not let the demons speak because they knew who he was.
>
> 35 **Very early in the morning, while it was still dark, Jesus got up, left the house and went off to a solitary place, where he prayed.** 36 Simon and his companions went to look for him, 37 and when they found him, they exclaimed: 'Everyone is looking for you!'
>
> 38 Jesus replied, 'Let us go somewhere else – to the nearby villages – so I can preach there also. That is why I have come.' 39 So he traveled throughout Galilee, preaching in their synagogues and driving out demons." (Mark 1:33-39)

Overnight Jesus has gone from obscurity to rock-star-like fame. His ability to heal and cast out demons has ignited all of Galilee to rush to Capernaum with all their sick and troubled kinfolk. The disciples, too, are excited about their Master's new-found fame.

After an incredible evening of healing and exorcism, Jesus stays the night at Peter's home. But the next morning Jesus is nowhere to be found. Already, people are at the door looking for Jesus. My father needs healing. My child needs deliverance. Peter, I must see Jesus. Where is he?

So Peter and his friends organize a search party to find their newly-famous Friend. Jesus is up before morning light and seeks out a "solitary place" (NIV, KJV), a "desolate" (ESV), "deserted" (NRSV) place. It is described by two Greek words: *topos*, "place" (from which we get our word "topography"), and *erēmos*, an adjective "pertaining to being in a state of isolation, isolated, desolate, deserted" of an area "unfrequented, abandoned, empty."[3] Capernaum is built next to a sloping rocky beach at the north end of the Sea of Galilee. Above the town are low hills with canyons sloping down to intermittent creeks (wadis) to the east and west. The beach with its fishing boats wouldn't offer much quiet,

---

[3] *Erēmos*, BDAG 391, 1a. The word can also be used of desert or wilderness, in contrast to cultivated and inhabited country.

so I'm guessing Jesus hikes up the hill above the homes below and finds a spot where he can talk to his Father undisturbed and watch the morning sun rise over the lake.

Finally, the disciples find Jesus. "Everybody is looking for you!" they exclaim (vs. 37). They sound like Hollywood agents trying to acquaint a new actor with his responsibilities to his public, to his fans. No doubt, they go on to explain that Jesus is needed, that he should continue to heal the new crowds of sick people in town who are demanding his help.

Jesus' response seems to ignore their demands. "Let us go somewhere else – to the nearby villages – so I can preach there also. That is why I have come" (vs. 38). In his early-morning time with his Father, Jesus has been seeking guidance on what to do next. And his Father has apparently told him that it's now time to begin an itinerant preaching tour of all the Galilee villages to spread the message of the Kingdom.

Notice that Jesus' emphasis is first "preaching." Healing isn't primary, though it is important, since it flows from Jesus' mission to save and his compassion, and serves to authenticate his message. "Preach" (NIV, ESV, KJV), "proclaim the message" (NRSV) is the Greek verb *kērussō*, "to make public declarations, proclaim aloud."[4] In this case, the preaching seems to be similar to the teaching he had done in the Capernaum synagogue (vs. 21),[5] since he continues to preach in other area synagogues (vs. 39).

Going away to pray is an important pattern in Jesus' life, one that he seeks to demonstrate before his disciples for them to emulate. Luke's Gospel seems to focus on these.

"At daybreak Jesus went out to a solitary place...." (Luke 4:42)

"Jesus often withdrew to lonely places and prayed." (Luke 5:16)

"One of those days Jesus went out to a mountainside to pray, and spent the night praying to God." (Luke 6:12)

"Once when Jesus was praying in private and his disciples were with him, he asked them, 'Who do the crowds say I am?'" (Luke 9:18)

"He took Peter, John and James with him and went up onto a mountain to pray." (Luke 9:28b)

---

[4] *Kērussō*, BDAG 544, 2bβ.

[5] "Teach" the imperfect voice (repeated action in the past) of *didaskō*, "to provide instruction in a formal or informal setting, teach" (BDAG 241, 2a).

"One day Jesus was praying in a certain place. When he finished, one of his disciples said to him, 'Lord, teach us to pray, just as John taught his disciples.'" (Luke 11:1)

"Jesus went out as usual to the Mount of Olives, and his disciples followed him. On reaching the place, he said to them, 'Pray that you will not fall into temptation.' He withdrew about a stone's throw beyond them, knelt down and prayed." (Luke 22:39-41)

It is often difficult for Jesus to pray, to get away from the people who are demanding things from him, but he makes the effort. It is his characteristic pattern. Notice, however, that he doesn't necessarily exclude his disciples from these times of prayer. By example he is teaching them to seek the Father.

We see a similar passion in David.

"O God, You are my God;
Early will I seek You;[6]
My soul thirsts for You;
My flesh longs for You
In a dry and thirsty land
Where there is no water." (Psalm 63:1, NKJV)

To help you internalize and apply what you are learning from this study, I have included several Discussion Questions in each lesson. These are designed to help you think about and ponder the most important points. Don't skip these. It is best to write out your answers, whether you post them or not. However, you can post your answers – and read what others have written – by going to the online forum by clicking on the URL below each question. (Before you can post your answer the first time, you will need to register. You can find instructions at http://www.joyfulheart.com/forums/instructions.htm

Q1. (Mark 1:33-39) What pattern do you see emerging in Jesus' prayer life? Why do you think he spends Quiet Time with the Father before the day begins? How does

---

[6] "Early will I seek thee" (KJV), renders a verb formed from the noun *shahar*, "dawn." Modern translations take the dawn figuratively and render the Piel perfect of *shāhar*, as "seek earnestly" (NIV, ESV, NASB) (Victor P. Hamilton, TWOT #2369). Holladay renders the Qal as "be intent on," and the Piel (as in our verse) as "be intent on, inquire for, seek" (Hebrew Lexicon, p. 366, Piel 1).

this prepare him for his ministry? How did the disciple desires for Jesus differ from what Jesus felt impelled to do? (Mark 1:37-38) Why? Do you have a Quiet Time? What could you do to improve the quality of your time with God each day? http://www.joyfulheart.com/forums/topic/1763-q1-jesus-prayer-pattern/

Seeing What the Father Is Doing (John 5:17-20)

John's Gospel is the source of a second important passage that explains Jesus seeking his Father's voice. The context is a dispute with the Pharisees, who are accusing Jesus both of breaking the Sabbath by healing on this day of rest and of blasphemy over his claims to a special relationship with the Father.

> "[17] Jesus said to them, 'My Father is always at his work to this very day, and I, too, am working.' [18] For this reason the Jews tried all the harder to kill him; not only was he breaking the Sabbath, but he was even calling God his own Father, making himself equal with God. [19] Jesus gave them this answer: **'I tell you the truth, the Son can do nothing by himself; he can do only what he sees his Father doing, because whatever the Father does the Son also does.** [20] For the Father loves the Son and shows him all he does. Yes, to your amazement he will show him even greater things than these.'" (John 5:17-20)

To the Pharisees' claim that Jesus should cease healing for the Sabbath, Jesus replies:

> "My Father is always at his work to this very day, and I, too, am working." (vs. 17)

In other words, "My Father doesn't stop working on the Sabbath. Why should I?" That angers his enemies, since Jesus seems to put himself on the same plane as God and justifies breaking the Sabbath.

But look at Jesus' words another way. God is always working, even if we don't see it, even if we don't know about it. Certainly God is working in ways the Pharisees don't discern. Jesus' power is in discerning what the Father is doing – and then cooperating with the Father in that. Open our eyes, Lord!

The Son Can Do Nothing by Himself (John 5:19)

"I tell you the truth, the Son can do nothing by himself; he can do **only what he sees**[7] his Father doing, because whatever the Father does the Son also does." (John 5:19)

Verse 19 troubles us because Jesus claims that he can't do anything by himself. Why not? Isn't he the Son of God?

To understand this verse, we need to consider what the Bible teaches about the Trinity.[8] Our doctrine of the Trinity teaches us that each member of the Godhead is fully God. Paul points to Jesus' humility by which he voluntarily lays aside some of these prerogatives of divinity.

"Who, being in very nature God,

did not consider equality with God something to be grasped,

but made himself nothing,

taking the very nature of a servant,

being made in human likeness." (Philippians 2:6-7)

Moreover, there is a voluntary submission to the Father's leadership. In 1 Corinthians we read:

"Then the end will come, when he hands over the kingdom to God the Father after he has destroyed all dominion, authority and power. For he must reign until he has put all his enemies under his feet. The last enemy to be destroyed is death. For he 'has put everything under his feet.' Now when it says that 'everything' has been put under him, it is clear that this does not include God himself, who put everything under Christ. When he has done this, then the Son himself will be made subject[9] to him who put everything under him, so that God may be all in all." (1 Corinthians 15:24-28)

If Christ finally subjects himself to the Father, does this mean that he is somehow inferior? No. The doctrine of the Trinity declares that the Father and Son and Holy Spirit are equal in Person, but the Son and Holy Spirit are subordinate to the Father in role – "ontological

---

[7] "Sees" is *blepō*, "see" (with the eye), then, by extension, "discern," here, perhaps in the sense of "to pay especially close attention to something, notice, mark something" (BDAG 179, 4).

[8] For more on the Trinity, read my article: "Four Reasons Why I Believe in the Trinity" (www.joyfulheart.com/scholar/trinity.htm).

[9] "Subjected" (NIV), "made subject" (NRSV), "subdued" (KJV) is *hypotassō*, "to cause to be in a submissive relationship, to subject, to subordinate" (BDAG 1042, 1a). Used three times in verse 1 Corinthians 15:28.

equality, but economic subordination," in other words, "equal in being, but subordinate in role."[10] This understanding of equality and role is apparent in the very words "Father" and "Son."

So the phrase, "the Son can do nothing by himself," indicates how dependent Jesus is upon the Father, especially during his time as a human being. As you study the Trinity, you see that members of the Godhead are interdependent, working together. For example, God creates the world through the agency of the Son (John 1:3; Colossians 1:16-17; Hebrews 1:2). The concept of independent action is foreign to the Godhead of Father, Son, and Holy Spirit.

I know this is getting theological, but it is important to what I'll say next.

Jesus' Reliance on the Father's Voice (John 5:19)

Historically, there are two basic ways Christians have explained Jesus' miracles:

1. **Jesus does miracles by virtue of being divine**. If this were true, Jesus' life is completely unique and can't serve as a useful example for us humans today. Moreover, Jesus would be unable to train his disciples to do as he did in ministry, since his actions would be due solely to his divinity.
2. **Jesus does miracles by the power of the Spirit**. In his humanness, Jesus performs miracles in the same way that he teaches his disciples to do them – by direction from and dependence upon the Father."[11]

I believe that this latter interpretation is much more faithful to John 5:19 than the "Jesus-works-miracles-because-he-is-divine" understanding. And it has huge implications in how we apply the patterns of the New Testament to our lives and ministry.

If we accept that Jesus' miracles resulted (at least in part) from him being a human being who is full of faith and in tune with his Father's will and timing, then Jesus becomes our exemplar as the Spirit-Filled Man, from whom we can learn how to operate in the Spirit!

---

[10] Wayne Grudem, *Systematic Theology* (Zondervan, 1994), pp. 251-252.

[11] Cessationists" believe that the miraculous gifts of the Holy Spirit ceased after the apostolic era, so for them, Jesus' miracle-working ministry is not a useful example. I am a "continuationist," not a "cessationist" because I see the whole New Testament as a pattern for disciples today, not just the "non-supernatural" portions of it. For a balanced description of this debate, read the "Cessationism versus Continuationism" article in Wikipedia.

Since, as Jesus says, God is always working, then he is always at work in our day, and if we can discern what he is doing – and cooperate with Him in it – then we will see the power of God in action through us.

Later in the same chapter, Jesus says something similar:

> "By myself I can do nothing; **I judge only as I hear**, and my judgment is just, for
> I seek not to please myself but him who sent me." (John 5:30)

So Jesus seeks to *see* what the Father is doing (verse 19) and *hear* what the Father is saying (verse 30). And on that basis, he acts.

God hasn't stopped working or speaking. Our job as twenty-first century Christians – as our brothers and sisters in centuries gone by – is to discern what he is doing, and then be his hands and feet in our generation.

Q2. (John 5:19, 30) Why do you think Jesus said, "By myself I can do nothing"? (vs. 30). How do you justify this statement with Jesus' divine nature as the Son of God? In what ways can we use Jesus' example as a pattern for our own life and ministry? How do you think Jesus would "see" and "hear" the Father?
http://www.joyfulheart.com/forums/topic/1764-q2-seeing-the-father/

Jesus' Pattern of Communing with the Father

Now that we've examined a passage describing Jesus' practice of going to a solitary place to pray (Mark 1:33-39) *and* a passage about his utter dependence upon communicating with the Father (John 5:19, 30), let's put them together and draw a conclusion.

I believe that Jesus patterns for his disciples a life of spending time in prayer away from the crowds so that he can talk to and listen to his Father about directions for his day and ministry. No doubt he talks with the Father throughout the day also, but it is Jesus' practice of getting away to pray that characterizes his prayer life in Luke's Gospel especially. Jesus shows his disciples how ministry is done by living it out before them

We, too, need to seek a meaningful time alone with God each day – preferably at the beginning of the day – to commune with God, not just to read Scripture (which we *must* do), but also to listen for God's whispers so that we might be ready for the day he brings to us. This is part of the "abiding" that Jesus talks about in the Parable of the Vine and the Branches (John 15:1-9). More about that in this lesson's assignment below.

Healing the Demon-Oppressed Boy (Mark 9:29)

Before we leave Jesus' example, let's look at one more incident in his life – the healing of the demon-oppressed boy. Jesus has just come down from the Mount of Transfiguration with Peter, James, and John, but when he arrives where his disciples are stationed, all he finds is utter confusion.

A father has brought his boy to the disciples to heal him from seizures caused by demonic activity. The disciples are unsuccessful in delivering the boy, and now there is an argument going on with the teachers of the law. After Jesus hears the father's story, he responds with impatience towards the unbelief he finds in the father – and probably in the teachers of the law. Jesus rebukes the demon and the boy is delivered. Later, the disciples ask Jesus why they couldn't cast out the demon in this case. Apparently they had had some previous successes in exorcism (Mark 3:15; 6:13; Luke 10:17). Jesus responds:

"This kind can come out only through prayer." (Mark 9:29)

Most early copies of the New Testament read "only through prayer and fasting," though it is clear that some of the best early manuscripts leave out the words "and fasting." Bible scholars believe it is "virtually certain" that the increased emphasis on fasting in the second or third century church induced scribes to add "and fasting" in verse 29.[12] It doesn't appear that Jesus' disciples practiced fasting beyond what was prescribed in the Law (Mark 2:18-20), nor do we read of Jesus himself fasting, except for the 40 days of his Wilderness Temptation.

So what does Jesus mean, "This kind can come out only through prayer"? Does he mean *regular* prayer? Certainly the disciples engaged in prayer as they followed Jesus on his journey. So it isn't likely that he is rebuking complete prayerlessness.

We know that "only through prayer" does not refer to Jesus' method of exorcism. Jesus never prays aloud when he cast out demons; rather he speaks a word of command.

I believe that "only through prayer" refers to the time Jesus spends with his Father in prayer. This isn't just a rote prayer or prayer lists – though these can be good. Jesus goes further; he talks to and listens to his Father in prayer. And through these regular times of prayer, Jesus knows how to deal with this particular demon. Perhaps, Jesus speaks a silent

---

[12] Metzger (*Textual Commentary*, p. 101) assesses the likelihood that "and fasting" was *not* in the original text of Mark with a "virtually certain" {A} designation. The words are missing only in Aleph*, B 0274 k; and Clement of Rome (95 AD), but these omissions occur across three of the major manuscript families (Alexandrian, Western, and Caesarean), increasing the likelihood that "and fasting" was a later addition. The words "prayer and fasting" also occur in Matthew 17:21, which appears to have been assimilated by scribes from Mark 9:29. Matthew 17:21 is rightly left out of modern translations of the New Testament.

"arrow prayer" to the Father and receives an instant response – "This is how to proceed in this situation." We're not sure. But it seems that the *quality* of Jesus' prayer life with the Father is what gives him power to deal with whatever situation presents itself.

Jesus Ministered in the Power of the Spirit

To understand the power of Jesus' ministry, we have to understand that he is empowered by the Third Person of the Trinity, the Holy Spirit. Luke's Gospel makes this clear.

"The **Holy Spirit descended on him** in bodily form like a dove." (Luke 3:22)

"Jesus, **full of the Holy Spirit**, returned from the Jordan and was led by the Spirit in the desert." (Luke 4:1)

"Jesus returned to Galilee **in the power of the Spirit**, and news about him spread through the whole countryside. He taught in their synagogues, and everyone praised him." (Luke 4:14-15)

"**The Spirit of the Lord is on me**,
because he has anointed me to preach good news to the poor.
He has sent me to proclaim freedom for the prisoners
and recovery of sight for the blind,
to release the oppressed,
to proclaim the year of the Lord's favor."
(Luke 4:18-19, quoting Isaiah 61:1-2)

Exactly how the Father, Son, and Holy Spirit work together during Jesus' earthly ministry is a mystery, though there are hints throughout the Gospels.

Christian believers, too, engage all three Persons of the Trinity. We are to pray to the Father in Jesus' name (John 16:26-27). Jesus promises to be with us always (Matthew 28:20). And we are promised the presence and gift of the Holy Spirit who mediates God to us here on earth (John 14-16). How this all fits together is again a mystery. Nevertheless, countless modern-day disciples have learned to live their lives in the presence of the Father, Son, and Holy Spirit.

Promises of the Holy Spirit (John 14-16)

We've observed Jesus' prayer life and ministry. Now we observe Jesus' teaching about the Holy Spirit and ministry.

Just before his crucifixion, Jesus teaches his disciples to expect the Holy Spirit to take a powerful role in their lives in the near future. I hesitate to go into great detail, or we'll be sidetracked from our main topic of listening for God's voice,[13] but this is important to our understanding of God's voice.

Jesus refers to the Spirit as the "Paraclete" (Greek *paraklētos*), translated variously as "Counselor" (NIV, RSV), "Advocate" (NRSV), "Helper" (ESV, NRSV, NKJV), "Comforter" (KJV), and "Friend" (*The Message*). *Paraklētos* is an adjective formed from the verb *parakaleō*, which has the basic meaning, "call to one's side" for help.[14] In Greek, the word can have the idea of one who provides help as a legal advocate, especially an advocate for the defense. Another approach might be "Friend," as in a Friend at court.[15]

In a fascinating passage, Jesus says that the Father will send "another Counselor" (*paraklētos*, John 14:16). Jesus has been their Paraclete, Helper, Friend thus far, but the Holy Spirit will replace Jesus as an interior presence, always with them, to guide and instruct them. The Holy Spirit, when he comes will be an "interior" Paraclete to be with them, Jesus tells them, "for he lives with you and will be in you" (John 14:17b). With reference to our topic of God's voice, Jesus promises that the Holy Spirit will:

1. Guide disciples into the way of truth (John 16:13).
2. Teach the disciples (John 14:26).
3. Speak to the disciples what the Spirit hears from the Father (John 16:13a).
4. Declare to the disciples what is to come (John 16:13b).

We've only scratched the surface here, but the time you spend studying John 14-16 will be richly rewarded in understanding the Spirit whom Jesus and the Father have given you. In short, the Holy Spirit is God's presence to guide, help, lead, and counsel us. Notice the promise of the Spirit speaking:

> "But when he, the Spirit of truth, comes, he will guide you into all truth. He will not **speak** on his own; he will **speak** only what he hears, and he will **tell you** what is yet to come." (John 16:13)

Of course, the Holy Spirit guides and inspires the apostles as they seek to understand doctrine and to record it in the Scriptures. But the Holy Spirit also "speaks" in non-revelatory ways, especially in the book of Acts (Acts 8:29; 10:19; 11:12; 13:2; 21:11). More on that later. In short, the Holy Spirit is our Counselor to whom we can go for help and guidance.

---

[13] For more on this, see my book, *John's Gospel: A Discipleship Journey with Jesus* (JesusWalk Publications, 2015).
[14] *Parakaleō*, BDAG 764-765.
[15] Liddell-Scott, *Greek-English Lexicon*.

Q3. (John 14-16) What promises concerning the Paraclete – Comforter – Counselor – Helper – Holy Spirit does Jesus give in John chapters 14-16? How do these relate to guidance? To "hearing" God?
http://www.joyfulheart.com/forums/topic/1765-q3-the-holy-spirit/

The Spirit Reveals the Mind of Christ (1 Corinthians 2:9-11, 16)

In an amazing passage where Paul extols the grace of God to reveal God to man, he quotes Isaiah 64:4 and Isaiah 40:13, and then contrasts them with the amazing era of the Spirit in which we live.

> [9b] "'No eye has seen, no ear has heard,
> no mind has conceived what God has
> prepared for those who love him' —

[10] 'but God has revealed it to us by his Spirit. **The Spirit searches all things**, even the deep things of God. [11] For who among men knows the thoughts of a man except the man's spirit within him? In the same way no one knows the **thoughts of God** except the Spirit of God....

> [16] 'For who has known the mind of the Lord
> that he may instruct him?'

But we have **the mind of Christ**." (1 Corinthians 2:9-11, 16)

The Holy Spirit can reveal God's thoughts and Christ's mind to believers today!

The word "mind" is *nous*, which doesn't mean "brain," since the ancients didn't understand that physical organ in the way we do today. Rather *nous* refers to "the faculty of intellectual perception, mind, understanding." Here, our verse may have the nuance, "result of thinking, mind, thought, opinion."[16]

Who can know God's thoughts? Who has the temerity to think he can tell God something God doesn't already know? No one. Isaiah's prophecy (quoted in 1 Corinthians 2:9-10) refers to the era of the Law before the Spirit comes to indwell the believer. Now things are different. We have the Holy Spirit who can communicate and mediate our thoughts at their most basic level and communicate to our spirits God's guidance and truth.

Does this mean that we now clearly understand God? No. We just get a glimpse, a word, a thought, so we shouldn't get cocky.

---

[16] *Nous*, BDAG 680, 3.

There's a story from India about a group of blind men who have never encountered an elephant before. Each feels a different part of the elephant's body – one a foot, another a tusk, etc., and then describes the elephant based on their partial, limited experience. No wonder their descriptions differ! Paul says,

> "Now we see but a poor reflection as in a mirror; then we shall see face to face. Now I know in part; then I shall know fully, even as I am fully known." (1 Corinthians 13:12)

There will come a time when it will all be clear, as the Book of Revelation puts it, "They will see his face" (Revelation 22:4a). Until then we get words, promptings, glimpses to help us forward.

Q4. (1 Corinthians 2:9-16) How does the Holy Spirit make "the mind of Christ" available to us? How does this make you dependent upon the Holy Spirit? How does this relate to listening for God's voice?
http://www.joyfulheart.com/forums/topic/1766-q4-mind-of-christ/

God Speaking to Believers is a Clear Biblical Pattern

We've considered Jesus' dependence on the Father as a deliberate pattern that Jesus is demonstrating for his disciples to follow. We've looked Jesus' promises to send the Holy Spirit as a Counselor and Helper. And we've considered how the Holy Spirit mediates access for us to Christ's very mind and thoughts.

Now I'd like to further assert that God speaking to individual believers is a clear Bible pattern intended for us to expect as the norm. True, in the Bible, God doesn't seem to speak to everyone. Nor does he speak constantly to those to whom he speaks. But I don't think you can look at the record of the Old and New Testaments and conclude anything else except that God speaks to people – leaders, prophets, and normal believers as well. Here's a partial list to help jog your memory:

- Moses
- Samuel
- David
- Gideon
- Simeon
- Paul

- Philip the Evangelist
- Ananias
- and many, many others.

There is a small group of well-meaning evangelicals, seeking to defend the doctrine of the Sufficiency of Scripture, who would insist that in our day we shouldn't expect God to speak as in Bible days. We should only expect God to speak by "quickening Scripture" to us.[17] Indeed, the Holy Spirit *does* "quicken Scripture"! However, to insist that we can't trust the Bible pattern to guide us in how we should expect God to speak to us today seems strange.

I can't help but conclude – if the Bible is to be our guidebook to Christian living – that God wants to continue speaking to his people today.

Lessons for Disciples

We've covered a lot of ground. Let's sum up the lessons for disciples that we've uncovered so far.

1. Jesus set a pattern for his disciples to talk to the Father in the morning in a solitary place (Mark 1:35; Luke 4:42; 5:16; 6:12; 9:18; 9:28b).
2. In Jesus' talks with his Father he received instructions for ministry (Mark 1:38).
3. Jesus depends on his Father for direction, and then acted on what he saw the Father do (John 5:19) and say (John 5:30).
4. God is always working (John 5:17), even if we're not aware of it.
5. Jesus' miracles are the result of the power of the Holy Spirit, not because of his unique divinity, since he had divested himself of many of his prerogatives of divinity when he became a human being (Philippians 2:6-7; Luke 3:22; 4:1, 14-15, 18-19).
6. The ability to cast out "difficult" demons comes from a life of prayer, which the disciples lacked early in their ministry.
7. In the Paraclete passages of John 14-16, Jesus promises that the Holy Spirit will: (a) guide disciples into way of truth (John 16:13); (b) teach the disciples (John 14:26); (c) speak to the disciples what the Spirit hears from the Father (John 16:13a); and (d) declare to the disciples what is to come (John 16:13b).

---

[17] People who hold this are usually "cessationists," who believe that the supernatural gifts of the Holy Spirit ceased with the death of the apostles and with the development of the New Testament canon of Scripture.

8. The Holy Spirit mediates to us the mind of Christ (1 Corinthians 2:9-11, 16).
9. There is a clear Bible pattern of God speaking to people in both the Old and New Testaments.

Week 1 Assignment. Set Aside a Regular Quiet Time to Spend with God

Since we're trying to develop a skill of listening for God's voice, each lesson includes a practical assignment for you to put into practice in your life that week. This is not an academic study of Bible theory, but a practical study that will result in your life being changed. So, here we go. If you'd like to see all the assignments together, so you can see where we're going, go to Appendix 2. Assignments to Sensitize You to God's Voice

Assignment 1: As a way of patterning yourself after Jesus, who sought the Father early and often, set aside for yourself a regular Quiet Time to spend with God. You may be already doing this. If so, great. But even if you already do this, it's time to "up your game," to renew this time so it is most meaningful.

Set aside at least five to ten minutes a day – or more, depending on your schedule – preferably in the morning when you have your whole day ahead of you.

Your Quiet Time is a time to touch base with your Friend and renew your relationship with him each day. It is also a discipline that serious Christians set up in their lives – whether they feel like it or not. Sometimes you'll be sluggish and not very spiritually in tune. Have your Quiet Time anyway; that's when you need it the most. Sometimes your Quiet Time may seem like just going through the motions. Do it anyway. Sometimes God meets you wonderfully in your Quiet Time. Rejoice!

Here's a simple guideline for a Quiet Time.[18]

1. **Greeting**. "Good morning, Father," is the way I often begin.
2. **Praise**. The Psalmist encourages us: "Worship the LORD with gladness; come into his presence with singing (Psalm 100:2; NRSV). Offer verbal praise: "Lord, I come before you with thanksgiving and praise this morning." Perhaps sing a praise chorus.
3. **Scripture.** Ask God to open his Word to you. Then read a portion of Scripture, not just a verse from a devotional guide. But read systematically. You might begin with the Gospel of Mark or the Gospel of John and read a chapter a day. Each day, pick up from where you left off the day before. I try to read a chapter from the Old Testament, a Psalm, and a chapter from the New Testament each day. There's no

---

[18] For more see my article, "Apply Fertilizer Liberally." www.joyfulheart.com/maturity/fertil.htm

right or wrong way here. However, whatever your practice is, stick with it – and don't coddle yourself! Over time, this regularity makes you acquainted with the whole Word of God. This helps you know the lines along which God is thinking, his values, and what pleases him. Then as God begins to speak or prompt you, you'll be able to discern whether it is God or not.

4. **Prayer.** There's an acronym ACTS – Adoration, Confession, Thanksgiving, Supplication – that is a useful guide. I confess my sins to God, and ask him to cleanse me (1 John 1:9). Then I bring before the Lord each of the people close to me and ask God to help them. Sometimes as I'm praying for someone, God will prompt me with some way I can minister to him or her.

5. **Listening.** We'll amplify this step in Lesson 2.

6. **Take notes.** Some people call this "journaling." It doesn't have to be formal, but be prepared to write down what God seems to be showing you.

Sometimes my pattern for my Quiet Time seems to grow stale. Then I mix it up, perhaps reading a devotional book along with scripture and prayer. Perhaps spending more time singing. At least for a while. Then I usually return to my usual pattern after a few weeks.

Over the years I've observed that people who have a regular Quiet Time are the ones who grow as disciples. Greg Krieger sees spiritual disciplines such as a Quiet Time as a way of putting up all the sails to catch the slightest breeze of the Spirit's whisperings.

Setting up a daily Quiet Time is your assignment for this week. Then talk to your spiritual partner and explain what your plan is. Later in the week, share how this is going. It's easier to form new habits when you have some accountability built in.

Prayer

Father, we are grateful for the example Jesus set for us in talking to you and listening to you, and then acting. Help us to seek you earnestly, listen to you carefully, and then act faithfully in the ways you are showing us. In Jesus' name, we pray. Amen.

Key Verses

"Very early in the morning, while it was still dark, Jesus got up, left the house and went off to a solitary place, where he prayed." (Mark 1:35, NIV)

"I tell you the truth, the Son can do nothing by himself; he can do only what he sees his Father doing, because whatever the Father does the Son also does." (John 5:19, NIV)

"By myself I can do nothing; I judge only as I hear, and my judgment is just, for I seek not to please myself but him who sent me." (John 5:30, NIV)

"His disciples asked him privately, 'Why could we not cast it out?' And he said to them, 'This kind cannot be driven out by anything but prayer.'" (Mark 9:28-29, NIV)

"God has revealed it to us by his Spirit. The Spirit searches all things, even the deep things of God…. We have the mind of Christ." (1 Corinthians 2:10, 16b, NIV)

2. Recognizing God's Voice (1 Kings 19)

We've established that hearing God's voice is a pattern throughout the Old and New Testaments. Seeking the Father early in the morning to get his marching orders for the day is the pattern that Jesus lived before his disciples. But what kind of voice should we expect?

God does speak to his disciples in words and sentences, which we'll consider in this lesson. He also speaks and leads by nudges, promptings, and in other ways (which we'll explore in Lesson 3).

'St. Elias' (10th or 11th century AD), icon in St Elias Monastery (Greek Orthodox), Shwayya, Lebanon

But for now, let's examine God's voice that comes in words and sentences by looking at a well-known Old Testament passage where Elijah hears God's voice on Mt. Sinai as a "still small voice," a voice that is preceded by – and contrasted to – ferocious wind, earthquake, and fire. After we consider Elijah, we'll look at other Bible instances of God speaking to his servants in clear words filled with direction or comfort.

Elijah's Great Victory and Deep Depression (1 Kings 17-19)

The prophet Elijah appears during the reign of Ahab, who is king of the northern kingdom from 875 to 852 BC. Ahab and his wife Jezebel have led the nation deep into the worship of Baal. Jezebel isn't Jewish, but Phoenician, and fanatically promotes the pagan fertility god Baal and his female consort Asherah. She personally supports 450 prophets of Baal and 400 prophets of Asherah (1 Kings 18:19). Ahab has systematically killed all of God's prophets that he can find. Elijah the prophet has declared a drought and has been in hiding for years.

Elijah personally challenges Ahab to a public contest on Mt. Carmel to see who will accept a sacrifice by fire – Baal or Yahweh. On the appointed day, all morning long and far into the afternoon, the prophets of Baal try every way they can to get Baal to answer them, but to no avail. Then Elijah builds an altar and sacrifices a bull on it. Immediately, God's fire falls and consumes the sacrifice – and even the stones of the altar. All the people fall to the ground and acknowledge Yahweh as the true God. Elijah slays the false prophets, and then calls on Yahweh to end a three year drought. God answers with a deluge. It is a clear, ringing victory for both Yahweh and his prophet Elijah.

But when Jezebel learns that her favorite religion has been discredited and her prophets killed, she threatens Elijah with death. Elijah runs for his life, all the way south to Beersheba, in the southern desert of Judah. Then he leaves his servant there and goes out into the wilderness a day's journey. The Scripture records:

> "[Elijah] went a day's journey into the desert. He came to a broom tree, sat down under it and prayed that he might die. 'I have had enough, LORD, he said. 'Take my life; I am no better than my ancestors.' Then he lay down under the tree and fell asleep." (1 Kings 19:4-5)

A psychologist might conclude that Elijah is suffering from depression. He has many of the symptoms: exhaustion from years of stress, no remaining energy, no zeal, sleeping except to take food, then sleeping again. He is filled with fear. He has isolated himself from people, leaving his servant behind in Beersheba. He has gone into the desert to die.

Elijah has lost hope. His lifework as a prophet seems to have amounted to nothing, in spite of spectacular, though temporary, victories. Twice, when Yahweh asks what he is doing there, he offers the same self-pitying complaint:

> "I have been very zealous for the LORD God Almighty. The Israelites have rejected your covenant, broken down your altars, and put your prophets to death with the sword. I am the only one left, and now they are trying to kill me too." (1 Kings 19:10, 14)

He measures his own personal worth by his accomplishments and has come up short. "I am no better than my ancestors" (verse 4b). Elijah is in sad shape.

The Theophany to Elijah (1 Kings 19:11-13)

It is fascinating and instructive to see how gently God restores his broken servant Elijah. An angel meets him in the desert and feeds him, then feeds him again. There's no scolding, no blaming.

After a forty-day journey on foot Elijah arrives at Mt. Horeb, another name for Mt. Sinai. "There he went into a cave and spent the night" (verse 9a). Rice suggests that the translation might be better, "the cave," since a definite article is used in Hebrew, suggesting that this was a famous or well-known cave. Perhaps it was the "cleft in the rock" on Mt. Sinai where Moses had seen God hundreds of years before (Exodus 33:22).[19]

The technical name for an appearance of God is a "theophany." It is clear from this passage that the author wants his readers to see Elijah's encounter in the light of Moses' experience on Mt. Sinai. Here are the main points of comparison:

Elijah (1 King 19:9-13)	Moses (Exodus 33:18-23)
"The **cave**." (vs. 9)	"A **cleft** in the rock." (vs. 22)
"Go out and stand on the mountain in the presence of the LORD…." (vs. 11a)	"There is a place near me where you may stand on a rock." (vs. 21)
"The LORD is about to **pass by**…." (vs. 11b)	"When my glory **passes by**, I will put you in a cleft in the rock and cover you with my hand until I have **passed by**." (vs. 22)
"[Elijah] pulled his cloak over his face and went out and stood at the mouth of the cave." (vs. 13a)	"My face must not be seen." (vs. 23b)

But now we see a difference. When God appears to Moses, he speaks the divine name Yahweh, and recounts his characteristics of mercy and justice (Exodus 33:19; 34:6-7). But when God appears to Elijah it is in a still small voice.

The author lists in a very structured way the things that God is *not* in (verses 11-12)

"A great and strong wind…   but the LORD was not in the wind.

An earthquake   but the LORD was not in the earthquake.

A fire   but the LORD was not in the fire.

And after the fire the sound of a low whisper." (NIV)

Clearly, the author is trying to make a point by contrasting the "low whisper" with the loud and spectacular displays of wind, earthquake, and fire. What's the point? Probably that God's presence is best conveyed in personal communication with his servants, not in some showy, spectacular display of power. The essence of God's nature is not power – though God is fully capable of displaying overwhelming power. Rather, the essence of God is in his relationship and communication to the person. In New Testament terms you

---

[19] Gene Rice, *Nations under God: A Commentary on the Book of 1 Kings* (International Theological Commentary; Eerdmans, 1990), pp. 158-161.

might say, "God is love" (1 John 4:8) or perhaps, "In the beginning was the Word, and the Word was with God and the Word was God" (John 1:1).

God certainly shows love to Elijah, even though Elijah's confidence has faltered. God restores him gently.

1. Yahweh asks him, "What are you doing here, Elijah" (vss. 9, 13), and then listens patiently to Elijah's self-pity without rebuke.

2. Yahweh reveals himself in his gentle voice. When God cares enough to talk to us personally, we know he loves us. He could scare us to death with his power, but instead he seeks to engage us with his voice.

3. Yahweh gently tells Elijah, "go back the way you came…." (vs. 15a). It's sometimes hard to go back after we have done embarrassing things, but it is an important part of our healing and restoration.

4. Yahweh gives Elijah new assignments (vss. 15-17).

5. Only after all this does Yahweh speak a gentle rebuke: By the way, you're not the only one left; I have 7,000 who have been faithful to me (vs. 18).

This gentle process of restoration reminds me of Jesus restoring Peter: "Do you love me, Peter? Feed my sheep" (John 21:15-19). Sometimes we're called to restore those who have failed or fallen. Gentleness, rather than harshness, is God's way.

> "Brothers, if someone is caught in a sin, you who are spiritual should restore him gently. But watch yourself, or you also may be tempted. Carry each other's burdens, and in this way you will fulfill the law of Christ." (Galatians 6:1-2)

The Still, Small Voice (1 Kings 19:12b)

We've considered the context of the Elijah passage. Now let's examine at the phrase that is often quoted with relation to the nature of God's voice – and rightly so. What do we learn from it? The phrase is variously translated:

"A gentle whisper." (NIV)
"The sound of a low whisper (ESV)
"A still small voice" (KJV)
"A light murmuring sound" (NJB)

"A sound of gentle blowing" (NASB)

"A sound of sheer silence"[20] (NRSV)

It can't mean *all* of these things! What can we make of it? The phrase consists of three Hebrew words:

1. *Qôl*, "voice, sound, noise."[21]
2. *Demāmâ*, "whisper," a rarely used word that denotes "calmness, stillness, silence, whisper," from *dāmam*, "be silent, still; wait."[22]
3. *Daq*, "thin, fine, gaunt," from *dāqaq*, "to crush, grind, break in pieces."[23]

While any of the popular translations shown above *could* be correct in their translation, I think "gentle whisper" (NIV), "sound of a gentle whisper" (ESV), or "still small voice" (KJV) are most likely – and helpful – since *qôl* is clearly a "voice" (rather than an undefined sound) in verse 13 that follows. "Murmuring" (NJB) or "blowing" (NASB) are interpretations rather than translations of the Hebrew words.

Learning from Elijah's Still Small Voice

There are several things to learn from this passage, though let's be careful not to assume that all manifestations of God's voice will be like Elijah experienced. For example:

1. God's voice is not always quiet. Sometimes it booms like the sound of many waters (Ezekiel 43:2; Revelation 1:15; 14:2; 19:6), thunder (John 12:28-29; Revelation 14:2), and loud trumpets (Hebrews 12:19; Revelation 1:10; 4:1).
2. God's voice is not always gentle. Sometimes it comes to bring a strong rebuke (Acts 26:14).

---

[20] Donald J. Wiseman, *1 and 2 Kings* (Tyndale Old Testament Commentary; Eerdmans, 1993) says, "'Stillness' is not incompatible with words for 'sound, voice' and the word 'thin' (*dāqqâ*)." So Rice (*1 Kings*, p. 160): "a filled, gripping perceptible, silence or stillness."

[21] *Qôl* primarily signifies a sound produced by the vocal cords (actual or figurative). In poetical passages (for the most part) the denotation embraces sounds of many varieties.... *qôl* should be distinguished from and compared to *hegeh*, *higgāyôn* (a low noise or utterance), *hāmôn* (a tumultuous, agitated noise or uttering), *rē'a*, *terû'âa* (a shout of alarm, or joy)" (TWOT #1998a). *Qôl* is used broadly: (1) 'sound, voice, call' of a man, sheep, flute; (2) 'noise, sound' of battle, ram's horn, words; (3) 'voice' of God (Holladay, p. 315).

[22] *Demāmâ*, TWOT #439a. Rice, *1 Kings*, p. 160. "'Calm' (of wind), cessation of any strong air movement, 'humming stillness' (1 Kg 19:12) (Holladay, p. 72). Elsewhere in the Old Testament the word is used only at Job 4:15-16 and Psalm 107:29.

[23] Herbert Wolf, TWOT #448b. Rice (*1 Kings*, p. 160) says, "*Daqqah* refers to that which has been reduced and made 'thin, fine, small,' but also may have the sense of 'soft, gentle.'" Holladay (p. 73) defines it as "'thin' – (1) scanty (hair, grain), (2) 'fine' of hoarfrost, dust, (3) 'lean' of cows, dwarfed, (4) 'soft' (quiet, 1 Kings 9:12)."

3. God's voice in not always even a voice or sound. Sometimes it is an impression, or a nudge, a dream or vision, as we'll explore in Lesson 3.

So let's not assume that Elijah's still small voice is *normative*. However, it is *common* among Christians, and beloved for a number of reasons.

1. God's voice is often quiet. Sometimes, unless you're trained to recognize God's voice, you might mistake it for a passing thought. I expect that sometimes God would like to talk to us, but too often we aren't listening. Or there is so much noise in our life and so little quiet, that God's gentle voice gets lost in the clutter.

Having said that, I know that God is fully capable of getting our attention if he needs to. But he would rather have us listen to him of our own volition. I have a three-year-old granddaughter who has developed a habit of "selective hearing." (We husbands can develop that, too.) Her mom will say something and she'll ignore it. Oh, I know that she heard it, because sometimes I'll ask her what her mother said, and she can usually repeat it. But she's not tuned in to listening and responding. Rather she's more intent on continuing to do whatever she's engaged in, or in whatever she can get away with. We can be like that with God.

It is quite possible that you've heard God's voice already, but didn't recognize it as such. It doesn't have to be loud or spectacular to be God.

2. God's voice can guide us in what to do. God gives Elijah an assignment to anoint three men – two kings and his prophetic successor.

I was once the interim pastor of a small church that, after a few months of my term, was acting increasingly dysfunctional. One of the leaders had a gripe about the regional denominational organization, and was trying to force the church to move its affiliation to another organization. When she realized that I wouldn't support this action, she began vicious a rumor campaign with the purpose of getting rid of me. It was difficult for me and others. The church was filled with tension. Half-truths and innuendos circulated unabated. Finally, I went to the Lord with a sort of cowardly prayer: "Lord, if you want to remove me from this assignment, it's okay with me." Before I had even finished my prayer, God spoke four words ever-so-clearly to my heart: "I want you here!" It brought great peace to me, as now I knew I was in God's will. Later in the week I found that my wife had received the same direction. We stayed. It was messy. But God brought health and stability – and eventually a new pastor – to that church.

Sometimes God's voice comes to clarify direction for us.

3. God's voice can provide comfort when we are anxious. Elijah is fearful and exhausted, depressed and hopeless. God comforts him by giving him new work to do – a new assignment. Jesus comforts and restores Peter in a similar way – with a mild rebuke – by asking him three times to care for his sheep, restoring him to his former ministry. As we'll see in a moment, God's word regarding Paul's thorn in the flesh is this kind of comforting word.

God also comforts Elijah by pointing him to a spiritual companion, Elisha, who will share his sometimes lonesome life with him, and eventually succeed him so that his life's work will continue after his passing. What a blessing!

4. God's voice can bring a rebuke. Sometimes, we need God to set us straight, to correct us and our errors of thinking. Elijah has been complaining, "I, only I, am left." God informs him that fully 7,000 people have not compromised their faith in Yahweh. And 7,000 may imply even more than the literal number. Seven is the number of completeness for the Hebrews, while 1,000 is their "big number," like "a million" is for Americans. So 7,000 may mean "a great many" people are still faithful to Yahweh.

We shouldn't be afraid of God's rebukes; rather, we should welcome them. The Proverbs reminds us:

> "My son, do not despise the LORD's discipline
> and do not resent his rebuke,
> because the LORD disciplines those he loves,
> as a father the son he delights in."
> (Proverbs 3:11-12; quoted in Hebrews 12:5-6)

God blesses us by leading us onto the right path when we've strayed – not something we should avoid.

When I was a new pastor, I found myself complaining that most of the men in the church didn't take their responsibility to maintain the church buildings, so I, the pastor, had to do it. Self-pity! Yet, there was a faithful member, Les Beyea, who did show up to help. One day, while I was complaining, God rebuked me with the seven words, "Shut up and let me bless you." I didn't understand it at the time, but I stopped complaining. Later, I realized that Les Beyea was God's tutor to teach me home maintenance and give me the confidence to add an addition to my home, and later build my own new house and supervise building classrooms and worship centers. God indeed was blessing me when I was complaining. God is amazing – and gracious!

Sometimes a word from God can combine comfort *and* rebuke. Once I was praying earnestly for one of my sons who had been wandering. I was praying based on my authority as his father, etc. On that occasion, God spoke six words to me: "He's my son too, you know." It was both a comfort that God had my son in his hands, as well as a gentle reminder that I didn't have to convince God of something that was clearly his desire too.

Q1. (1 Kings 17-19) Why do you think the author contrasts the "still small voice" to the wind, earthquake, and fire? How does God's voice comfort and renew Elijah? Why is it easy to miss God when his voice is gentle and quiet?
http://www.joyfulheart.com/forums/topic/1767-q1-still-small-voice/

Samuel Anointing David (1 Samuel 16:1-13)

We've looked at Elijah. Now let's turn to other servants of God. Samuel has full conversations with the Lord concerning his ministry assignments. For example, God tells Samuel just how to anoint a new king from among Jesse's sons without alerting Saul, who would kill him if he knew (1 Samuel 16:1-3).

When Samuel arrives in Bethlehem, Jesse lines up his sons before the prophet and Samuel goes down the line. You can see Samuel's own personal inclinations creeping into the selection.

> "When they arrived, Samuel saw Eliab and thought, 'Surely the LORD's anointed stands here before the LORD.' But the LORD said to Samuel, 'Do not consider his appearance or his height, for I have rejected him. The LORD does not look at the things man looks at. Man looks at the outward appearance, but the LORD looks at the heart.'" (1 Samuel 16:6-7)

God speaks directly to Samuel's mind. For each of the other sons, Samuel senses a "No" and goes on to the next. When God says "No" to all seven sons before him, Samuel asks Jesse if he has any more sons. Sure enough! Jesse sends for David. Then God says:

> "Rise and anoint him; he is the one." (1 Samuel 16:12b).

This seems to fit my own experience – an occasional clear sentence with important content. But more likely God's communication to me consists mainly of, "Talk to Mary," or "Yes, go ahead," or, "No, wait." We'll explore this further in Lesson 3.

But We're Not All Prophets

In the Old Testament, the phrase, "The word of the Lord came to...." was the sign that God had raised up a prophet. So far as we can see from Scripture, God's instructions to prophets were mostly in words. Word messages are common in the New Testament, as we'll see. (In addition, you'll often see in the Bible God speak words through dreams, visions, and angels. I'm not trying to be comprehensive here, just to point out some particular communications that we can learn from.)

I can anticipate your response: "But we're not prophets. We can't expect to hear God's word."

Not so fast.

When the Spirit falls on the 70 elders at Mt. Sinai, Moses muses, "Would that all God's people were prophets" (Numbers 11:29). Looking forward to the outpouring of the Spirit in the Messianic Age, Joel prophesies:

"And afterward, I will pour out my Spirit on all people.

Your sons and daughters will prophesy,

your old men will dream dreams, your young men will see visions.

Even on my servants, both men and women,

I will pour out my Spirit in those days." (Joel 2:28-29)

When the Spirit is poured out at Pentecost, Peter interprets the speaking in tongues by quoting this prophecy of Joel. As we noticed in Lesson 1, all God's people now have access to the Spirit – and therefore, as they seek him, to the mind of Christ. While we all can potentially utter prophecy on occasion (1 Corinthians 14:1, 5, 31), few will have the *ministry office* of prophet (1 Corinthians 12:28-30; Ephesians 4:11). Nevertheless, through the Spirit, the communication channel for God to speak to us (and through us) has been established for all God's children. We just need to learn how to use this new-fangled technology.

Words of Encouragement

The still small voice to Elijah brings comfort and restoration. Paul, too, receives several words of encouragement from the Lord over the course of his ministry. They are memorable – often short – but they provide him the assurance that he needs at the time.

Paul has a way of stirring his enemies to violence when he talks about Jesus and performs miracles in Jesus' name. The Jews persecute. The pagans get upset. Paul receives more than his share of violence – lashings, beatings, stonings, imprisonments (2

Corinthians 11:24-26). By the time he arrives in Corinth on his Second Missionary Journey, he is weary, and perhaps frightened, as the Jews begin to agitate the populace against him. Knowing his weakness and fear, God speaks to him in a night vision:

> "Do not be afraid; keep on speaking, do not be silent. For I am with you, and no one is going to attack and harm you, because I have many people in this city." (Acts 18:9-10)

Another time, Paul is afflicted with some kind of problem, "a thorn in my flesh, a messenger of Satan, to torment me" (2 Corinthians 12:7). There's lots of speculation about what it was. A person? A demon? I expect it was some kind of chronic physical ailment. We don't really know. In three extended sessions of prayer Paul pleads with God to take it away – without response. But then, God speaks to him a word, a sentence:

> "My grace is sufficient for you, for my power is made perfect in weakness." (2 Corinthians 12:9a)

Though the answer isn't what Paul wants, he is profoundly moved by it, because God has taught him a wonderful truth: He is strong when he depends on God. The result is that Paul begins to exult in his weakness (2 Corinthians 12:10). His whole attitude has been changed by a personal word from God.

In a third instance, Paul has been attacked and falsely accused by the Jerusalem Pharisees, who plan to kill him. As he sits in the Roman barracks, beat up and discouraged, God's speaks to him:

> "The following night the Lord stood near Paul and said, 'Take courage! As you have testified about me in Jerusalem, so you must also testify in Rome.'" (Acts 23:11)

As Paul senses the Lord's presence, he knows that he is not alone, that God has this all in hand, and that God has a plan he is working out for the future. Paul's wounds may still be aching, but his heart is lifted up. He has heard from God.

Finally, just before a shipwreck on his voyage to Rome, an angel brings him a word of assurance that he subsequently shares with the ship's crew:

> "Do not be afraid, Paul. You must stand trial before Caesar; and God has graciously given you the lives of all who sail with you." (Acts 27:24)

Q2. (1 Corinthians 12:9a; Acts 18:9-10; 23:11; 27:24) How do you think it feels to Paul for God to personally encourage him when he is afraid and hurting? What do we

learn about God that he speaks to Paul in this way?
http://www.joyfulheart.com/forums/topic/1768-q2-encouraging-word/

Guidance to Travel to Jerusalem – and Confusing Interpretations

The story of Paul traveling to Jerusalem at the conclusion of his Third Missionary Journey is instructive concerning God's voice. It begins with Paul seeing extraordinary miracles in Ephesus, with many people burning expensive occult books and turning to Christ (Acts 19:9-20).

> "Now after these events Paul resolved in the Spirit to pass through Macedonia and Achaia and go to Jerusalem, saying, 'After I have been there, I must also see Rome.'" (Acts 19:21, ESV).

If you didn't know better, you might think that Paul decides[24] on his own. The NIV interprets it this way, taking "spirit" as human spirit, rather than Holy Spirit.[25] But as the story progresses, we find that this isn't Paul's decision, but the Spirit's directive.

> "And now, compelled by the Spirit, I am going to Jerusalem, not knowing what will happen to me there." (Acts 20:22)

The phrase "compelled by the Spirit" (NIV), "as a captive to the Spirit" (NRSV), "constrained by the Spirit" (ESV), "bound in the spirit" (KJV), uses the Greek verb *deō*.[26] The verb means "to confine a person or thing by various kinds of restraints, bind, tie," here with the connotation of binding and imprisoning.[27] And the Greek syntax makes a specific contrast between "I" (Paul) and "the Spirit."[28] This isn't my choice, Paul is saying, it's the Spirit of God who compels me to go to Jerusalem at this time.

It's important that Paul knows God's direction for sure. Because it isn't long until various believers and prophets sense "in the Spirit" what will happen in Jerusalem –

---

[24] "Decided" (NIV), "resolved" (NRSV, ESV), "purposed" (KJV) is the very common verb *tithēmi*, "put, place," here, "have (in mind), resolve" (BDAG 1003, 1bε).

[25] Either "spirit" or "Spirit" is possible, since there are no capitals or lower-case in the early Greek manuscripts to tell you. The capitalizations in English Bibles are the translator's decision.

[26] *Deō* is in the perfect passive voice ("having been bound").

[27] *Deō*, BDAG 221, 1b. The sense is caught well in the NRSV translation, "as captive to the Spirit."

[28] The Greek uses the pronoun *egō*, "I" – usually omitted unless there is a specific point to make. "The Spirit" here has the definite article, "the Spirit," so Paul is deliberately setting up the contrast between "I" and "the Spirit."

imprisonment. And "in the flesh" they interpret this result as a reason why he shouldn't go there. He says to the Ephesian elders on the beach at Miletus:

> "And now, compelled by the Spirit, I am going to Jerusalem, not knowing what will happen to me there. I only know that in every city the Holy Spirit warns me that prison and hardships are facing me. I consider my life worth nothing to me, if only I may finish the race and complete the task the Lord Jesus has given me – the task of testifying to the gospel of God's grace." (Acts 20:22-24)

Paul is Jesus' witness, and he must go to testify wherever his Master sends him. When his ship reaches Caesarea, a Roman port on the coast of Palestine, towards the end of his journey, a well-known prophet named Agabus travels to meet him.

> "Coming over to us, he took Paul's belt, tied his own hands and feet with it and said, 'The Holy Spirit says, "In this way the Jews of Jerusalem will bind the owner of this belt and will hand him over to the Gentiles."'" (Acts 21:11)

The prophecy is accurate. But his friends try to dissuade him from going to Jerusalem. They conclude that God's will just *can't* include pain and suffering for the great apostle.

> "When we heard this, we and the people there pleaded with Paul not to go up to Jerusalem." (Acts 21:12)

The "flesh" resists pain and struggle. The "flesh" can keep us from doing what God tells us to do, if we're not sure of what God has told us.

> "Then Paul answered, 'Why are you weeping and breaking my heart? I am ready not only to be bound, but also to die in Jerusalem for the name of the Lord Jesus.' When he would not be dissuaded, we gave up and said, 'The Lord's will be done.'" (Acts 21:13-14)

And so Paul continues his journey to Jerusalem, and to inevitable imprisonment – Jesus' will for his beloved servant Paul. Paul's clear direction while in Ephesus keeps him from giving in to other people's desire for his safety.

Q3. (Acts 19:21; 20:22-24; 21:12-14) What would have happened if Paul hadn't been sure of his instructions from the Holy Spirit to go to Jerusalem? Would you have tried to dissuade him? It's comforting to receive encouraging words. What level of maturity does it take to receive a direction that might lead us into hardship and danger? What happens when we choose the easy way, when God leads us on a

difficult path?
http://www.joyfulheart.com/forums/topic/1769-q3-go-to-jerusalem/

Instruction to Testify in Rome (Acts 23:11)

We already considered the following verse as one of the Lord's words of encouragement to Paul. But I want us to see it in the context of the next phase of guidance. Paul is imprisoned in the Roman barracks in Jerusalem. Jesus says to him:

> "Take courage! As you have testified about me in Jerusalem, so you **must** also testify in Rome." (Acts 23:11)

Remember Paul's desire while still in Ephesus to visit Rome after he reaches Jerusalem?

> "After I have been there, I **must** also see Rome." (Acts 19:21b)

In Ephesus, he was guided by the Spirit to definitely go to Jerusalem, but the thought of Rome is there, as well. The "must" in both Acts 19:21b and 23:11 is the infinitive verb *dei*, "to be under necessity of happening, it is necessary, one must, one has to, denoting compulsion of any kind."[29] Now, in prison in Jerusalem, Jesus renews and clarifies that Rome is the next objective.

It takes two years in prison before the ship leaves for Rome with Paul on board, but Paul knows what's coming. He just doesn't anticipate all that intervenes in the meantime. For protection, Paul is taken to Caesarea, the Roman capital of the province of Judea and kept under guard in Herod's palace. For the next two years he has to deal with various kings and politicians.

Felix, the Roman governor, who leaves Paul in prison to do the Jews a favor – and hopes to receive a bribe (Acts 24:26-27).

Porcius Festus, Felix's successor as Roman governor, who wants to do the Jews a favor by asking Paul to answer charges in Jerusalem (where his enemies have vowed to assassinate him). To avoid a mock trial in Jerusalem, Paul exercises his right as a Roman citizen to have his case heard before the emperor Caesar (or his representative) in Rome. Paul utters the legal words: "I appeal to Caesar!," setting in motion his transfer to Rome (Acts 25:10-12).

Herod Agrippa (a Rome-appointed Jewish king of part of Palestine) and his wife Bernice, who discuss the case with Festus and hear Paul's testimony. They conclude:

---

[29] *Dei*, BDAG 214, 1. *Dei* is the infinitive of *deō*, "bind, tie," that we saw in Acts 20:22.

"'This man is not doing anything that deserves death or imprisonment.' Agrippa said to Festus, 'This man could have been set free if he had not appealed to Caesar.'" (Acts 26:31b-32)

This is all "politician talk." They know that there is no substance to a legal case against Paul. But both Festus and Agrippa want to please the Jewish religious leaders, so in reality, they have no intention of releasing him, even if he hadn't appealed to Caesar. Nevertheless, they blame his continued confinement on Paul's appeal to Rome so they can feel good about their injustice.

But God is at work in spite of the politicians. He has directed his servant Paul to be a **witness** for him.

"Take courage! As you have **testified** about me in Jerusalem, so you must also **testify** in Rome." (Acts 23:11)

Paul's arrest in Jerusalem actually enables Paul to give his **testimony** before:
- The crowd in the Jerusalem Temple (Acts 21:40-22:21).
- The Sanhedrin, the Jewish leaders (Acts 22:30-23:10).
- The high priest, elders, and Felix the Roman governor (Acts 24:1-21).
- Felix and his wife Drusilla, a Jewess (Acts 24:24-26).
- Festus the new Roman governor (Acts 25:6-12).
- Festus, King Agrippa, and his wife Bernice (Acts 26:1-29).
- The soldiers guarding him and the ship's crew on the voyage to Rome (Acts 27).
- The residents of Malta, and Publius, the Roman official of Malta where they shipwrecked (Acts 28:1-10).
- The Jewish community in Rome (Acts 28:17-28).
- The Praetorian guard in Rome, charged with guarding Paul (Philippians 1:12-14).
- Caesar, the Emperor himself (Acts 27:24).

All this comes about because Paul is sure enough of God's guidance that he obeys the Lord to travel to Jerusalem – despite the dangers – and disregards the counter-counsel of a New Testament prophet and the whole Christian community! And so Paul fulfills what the Lord has initially told Ananias:

"Go! This man is my chosen instrument **to carry my name** before the Gentiles and their kings and before the people of Israel. I will show him how much he must suffer for my name." (Acts 9:15-16; cf. Matthew 10:18)

What are we to learn from this? Be sure of what God tells you and then persist in it. God knows what he is doing. And Christ will do great things through you as you listen and obey.

The Embarrassment of Not Persisting

I've learned the hard way that God knows best. My wife and I were heavily involved in a political campaign to keep open a library in our community after the county's decision to close their library branch. As all this was evolving, God spoke to me during a spring church leadership retreat: "You won't be involved in the leadership of the library" (or something like that. I wish I had written it down!).

A few months later, with the future of the town's library secured, the town began to take applications for people to serve on the Library Board. I really *wanted* to be on the library board, so I began to second-guess what God had told me months before. Perhaps I misunderstood, I reasoned. So I submitted an application, fully expecting – and hoping – to be appointed. When others were appointed instead of me, I was hurt. Surely I was better qualified!

My pride and immature desire for recognition had drowned out God's word to me. As I realized this, I was deeply embarrassed. I knew better! I knew what God had said, yet I didn't cling to it. Fortunately, no great harm was done – except to my pride. But it taught me a lesson in humility and the importance of holding fast to what God tells me, even if I don't understand it.

Don't Hesitate to Go with Them (Acts 10)

Two clear examples from Scripture stand out to me of God speaking a definite word to direct a disciple's ministry.

The first concerns Peter. He is on a the roof praying in the coastal city of Joppa, when he has a trance and a dream. Three times he is commanded to eat unclean animals; when he refuses, the word comes: "Do not call anything impure that God has made clean." When he awakes from the trance, the lesson strong in his mind, and the Spirit speaks clearly to him:

> "Simon, three men are looking for you. So get up and go downstairs. Do not hes-
> itate to go with them, for I have sent them." (Acts 10:19b-20)

Sure enough, when he goes downstairs, there are the three men – Gentiles – and Peter agrees to go with them, beginning an adventure that leads to the evangelization of the Gentiles all over the known world.

Q4. (Acts 10:19-20) Why was it important for Simon to get a very clear command from the Spirit to go with his visitors? What would he have done if the word weren't so clear? What does he do when criticized for taking this action (Acts 11:2, 12)? What kind of faith does it take to obey the Spirit and take an action you know you'll be criticized for later? Do you disobey when you know you might face criticism for obedience?
http://www.joyfulheart.com/forums/topic/1770-q4-clear-direction/

Separate for Me Paul and Barnabas (Acts 13:1-3)

Another such word comes to group of believers gathered in Antioch:

"1 In the church at Antioch there were prophets and teachers: Barnabas, Simeon called Niger, Lucius of Cyrene, Manaen (who had been brought up with Herod the tetrarch) and Saul. 2 While they were worshiping the Lord and fasting, the Holy Spirit said, **'Set apart for me Barnabas and Saul for the work to which I have called them.'** 3 So after they had fasted and prayed, they placed their hands on them and sent them off." (Acts 13:1-3)

When God speaks to a group of people, we call it prophecy. There's not a whole lot of difference in the mechanism between prophecy and an individual hearing God's voice. In each case the Holy Spirit speaks something to a person in intelligible words. In the case of prophecy, the prophet relays that message to the group – often at the same time as it is being revealed to him or her.

I mention this because it is an example of a clear sentence from God that can provide direction in ministry.

Lessons for Disciples

Let's summarize some of the things we've learned as we've reviewed God's voice to his servants in words and sentences.

1. God doesn't always speak quietly; sometimes his voice is loud and strong.
2. God revealed himself to Elijah in a "still small voice" (1 Kings 19:12).

3. God's voice is often quiet. Thus we can easily miss his voice in the clutter of our minds, through "selective hearing," or mistake it as one of our own passing thoughts.

4. God's voice in words and sentences can guide us what to do.

5. God's voice can provide comfort when we are anxious.

6. God's voice can also set us on the right path with a gentle rebuke.

7. God's voice can correct our preconceptions, as God did when Samuel was seeking a king among Jesse's sons (1 Samuel 16:1-13).

8. God's voice doesn't come only to prophets (Numbers 11:29). Since the Holy Spirit was poured out on the whole church at Pentecost (Acts 2), all of us have the Holy Spirit, who provides access to God's message, even if we don't hold the ministry office of a prophet (1 Corinthians 14:1, 5, 31; 12:28-30; Ephesians 4:11).

9. God's voice can bring words of encouragement to us when we are afraid and discouraged as he did to Paul on several occasions (Acts 18:9-10; 2 Corinthians 12:9; Acts 23:11; 27:24).

10. God's voice can bring us clarity, even when others dispute what God has shown us to do. Paul had such clarity about traveling to Jerusalem, even though people warned him "in the Spirit" what would happen there (Acts 19:21; 20:22-24; 21:11-14). Paul also had clarity about testifying in Rome, though politicians tried to make his imprisonment sound like his own fault (Acts 19:21; 23:11).

11. We are wise to persist in what God has shown us and to resist second-guessing God because of our unsurrendered desires.

12. Words from God can also give us direction for ministry. Examples are Peter taking the Gospel to the Gentiles in Caesarea (Acts 10) and Paul and Barnabas embarking on their First Missionary Journey (Acts 13:1-3).

Week 2 Assignment. Learn to Quiet Yourself and Listen

One of the chief reasons we miss God's voice is because we don't take time to listen. We rush through our devotions and then we're off to work or making breakfast or dinner, or something. We don't take time to listen.

I've found that it's much easier to quiet myself at the *beginning* of the day, before I review my e-mail and read the news. Those activities get my mind going a mile-a-minute in all sorts of directions. So the best time to spend with God is before I begin the activities of the day, when the day is new and my spirit is fresh.

I understand that this doesn't work for everyone. If you're a new mother, for example, there may not be quiet at the beginning of the day. Or you may not be a "morning person." You'll need to find some work-arounds, different times of the day when you can take some minutes with God by yourself.

If there are people around, explain that you're going to be praying for a few minutes. Then withdraw into your own thoughts. The more you do this, the better you'll be at it.

Whatever time and place works best in your circumstances, know that one of the keys to hearing God is to quiet yourself before him. The Quakers call it "centering down," quieting one's mind and spirit before God. My pastor sings simple, repetitive praise songs. Some traditions repeat a prayer over and over again. Others recommend breathing in and out, listening to your breathing as a way of quieting your thoughts.

I usually focus my attention on God through praise and worship. I might sing a hymn or praise chorus, or read a psalm. I've found that when I read silently, my mind can wander to other things. But when I read aloud it's easier to keep focus. I find that as I spend a few minutes in worship, my thoughts become less scattered and become aligned with God's.

These are all techniques to quiet one's spirit. Don't get hung up on the virtues of one technique over another. Your purpose here is to get the swirling currents of your mind quieted all flowing in the same direction – towards God.

Once your spirit has become quiet, I encourage you to talk to God about what's going on in your life and listen.

"Be still, and know that I am God." (Psalm 46:10)

"The LORD is in his holy temple;
let all the earth be silent before him." (Habakkuk 2:20)

Your assignment this week is to practice quieting your spirit before the Lord so you can listen. Then talk to your mentor and/or spiritual partner about your experiences of quieting your spirit before God.

Prayer

Father, thank you for the gift of your Holy Spirit that enables us to have access to you, to your voice and to your thoughts. I pray that you'd help us to quiet ourselves before you so we can hear you as you speak to our hearts. Thank you for caring about me so much that you'd stoop to talking to me personally. And I know that you care just as much about my brothers and sisters who are studying this with me. Thank you! In Jesus' name, we pray. Amen.

Key Verses

"The LORD said, 'Go out and stand on the mountain in the presence of the LORD, for the LORD is about to pass by.' Then a great and powerful wind tore the mountains apart and shattered the rocks before the LORD, but the LORD was not in the wind. After the wind there was an earthquake, but the LORD was not in the earthquake. After the earthquake came a fire, but the LORD was not in the fire. And after the fire came a gentle whisper." (1 Kings 19:11-12, NIV)

"When they arrived, Samuel saw Eliab and thought, 'Surely the LORD's anointed stands here before the LORD.' But the LORD said to Samuel, 'Do not consider his appearance or his height, for I have rejected him. The LORD does not look at the things man looks at. Man looks at the outward appearance, but the LORD looks at the heart.' … 'Rise and anoint him; he is the one.'" (1 Samuel 16:6-7, 12b, NIV).

"And afterward, I will pour out my Spirit on all people.
Your sons and daughters will prophesy,
your old men will dream dreams, your young men will see visions.
Even on my servants, both men and women,
I will pour out my Spirit in those days." (Joel 2:28-29, NIV)

"Do not be afraid; keep on speaking, do not be silent. For I am with you, and no one is going to attack and harm you, because I have many people in this city." (Acts 18:9-10, NIV)

"My grace is sufficient for you, for my power is made perfect in weakness." (2 Corinthians 12:9a, NIV)

"Take courage! As you have testified about me in Jerusalem, so you must also testify in Rome." (Acts 23:11, NIV)

"Do not be afraid, Paul. You must stand trial before Caesar; and God has graciously given you the lives of all who sail with you." (Acts 27:24, NIV)

"Now after these events Paul resolved in the Spirit to pass through Macedonia and Achaia and go to Jerusalem, saying, 'After I have been there, I must also see Rome.'" (Acts 19:21, ESV)

"And now, compelled by the Spirit, I am going to Jerusalem, not knowing what will happen to me there." (Acts 20:22, NIV)

"Simon, three men are looking for you. So get up and go downstairs. Do not hesitate to go with them, for I have sent them." (Acts 10:19b-20, NIV)

"While they were worshiping the Lord and fasting, the Holy Spirit said, 'Set apart for me Barnabas and Saul for the work to which I have called them.'" (Acts 13:2, NIV)

3. Nudges and No (Acts 8:26-40; 16:6-10)

As we saw in Lesson 2, God is fully capable of speaking words and sentences to us to convey concepts. In my experience – and from our expectations based on the biblical record of how he relates to his people – he still does this today.

Over the fifty plus years I've been listening for God's voice, I have heard him speak in words perhaps a few dozen times. But most of the time it is in impressions, nudges, promptings, noes – many thousands of them, if I

Herbert Boeckl, 'Philip and the Ethiopian Eunuch,' (1952-60), Angel's Chapel, Seckau Abbey, Styria, Austria

were to count them all up. Perhaps the best way to describe this is as inarticulate impressions in my mind to do this or that – or *not* to do something. These are usually whispers that don't come articulated in the form of a complete sentence or even in words.

I believe you see this form of God's voice in Scripture too.

Philip and the Ethiopian Eunuch (Acts 8:26-40)

For example, let's examine God's guidance in the case of Philip and the Ethiopian Eunuch. Philip has been part of a revival in Samaria. Now he's ready for a new place of ministry.

> "Now an angel of the Lord said to Philip, "Go south to the road – the desert road – that goes down from Jerusalem to Gaza.'" (Acts 8:26)

The angel points Philip in a clear direction, probably in words, but perhaps just an impression. It just so happens that he sees coming towards him a chariot in which is seated an Ethiopian eunuch, the Queen's treasurer. And it just so happens that the man is trying to read a scroll of Isaiah 53 while riding in the bouncing chariot. Now there is another directive.

"The Spirit told Philip, 'Go to that chariot and stay near it.'" (Acts 8:29)

Philip obeys and starts jogging alongside the chariot. He engages the Ethiopian in conversation, is invited aboard the chariot, and begins to explain the Scripture to the man. Before long, the Ethiopian asks to be baptized at an oasis alongside the road and Philip complies. Then Philip disappears, only to find himself in Azotos (The Greek name for the coastal city of Ashdod), and travels north along the coast, preaching the gospel as he goes, until he reaches Caesarea.

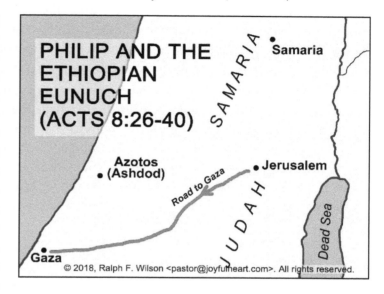

PHILIP AND THE ETHIOPIAN EUNUCH (ACTS 8:26-40)

What I see going on here are promptings, "nudges." Philip receives two nudges, the first from an angel:

1. **Go down to the road to Gaza.**

Once he gets there, he sees a chariot coming. Now comes the second nudge, this time from "the Spirit":

2. **Catch up with that chariot.**

I call these "nudges" because the messages don't contain much content to speak of, only a brief direction – "Gaza." Okay, God. Then, "chariot," as he glimpses the chariot. Okay, God. The author of Acts phrases these as sentences in order to communicate clearly to the readers, but the essence of the messages can be expressed in just a word or two.

Philip obeys these promptings, and then sees how God has set up the circumstances so he can win the official to Christ. God nudges him into the situation, and Philip takes it from there.

I've found this kind of nudge extremely common. In the Bible we see complete sentences, as if there is a spoken command. But other passages of Scripture – and my own experience – suggests that this is often a non-verbal nudge or impression from God.

Where to Preach – and Where Not To (Acts 16:6-10)

Let me give some further examples. Paul and Silas have begun their Second Missionary Journey and travel to encourage some of the churches established on Paul's First Journey. They get to Derbe and Lystra, where we pick up the narrative.

> "⁶ Paul and his companions traveled throughout the region of Phrygia and Galatia, having been kept by the Holy Spirit from preaching the word in the province of Asia. ⁷ When they came to the border of Mysia, they tried to enter Bithynia, but the Spirit of Jesus would not allow them to. ⁸ So they passed by Mysia and went down to Troas. ⁹ During the night Paul had a vision of a man of Macedonia standing and begging him, "Come over to Macedonia and help us." ¹⁰ After Paul had seen the vision, we got ready at once to leave for Macedonia, concluding that God had called us to preach the gospel to them." (Acts 16:6-10)

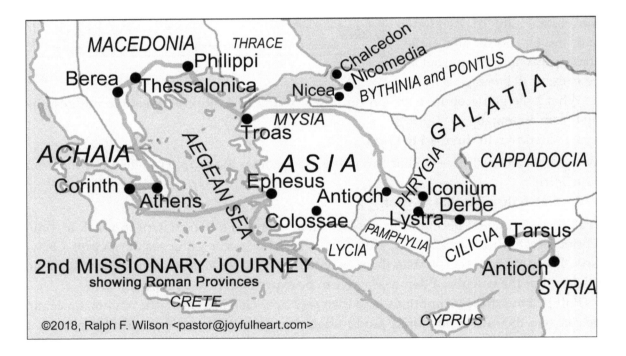

©2018, Ralph F. Wilson <pastor@joyfulheart.com>

(As you look at the map, you can see the boundaries of the Roman provinces. Contained within this provincial boundaries are ancient regions determined more by people groups than arbitrary borders. The region of Phrygia, for example, straddles both the Roman

Province of Asia and the Province of Galatia, and Mysia is contained within the Province of Asia.)

Here's how I reconstruct what's going on.

Don't preach in Asia (Acts 16:6). Their original plan, I am guessing, was to head for Ephesus, a major city and capital of the Roman Province of Asia. Paul and his party had been traveling the Via Sebaste (Imperial Road, Roman Road) constructed by the Romans beginning in 6 BC.[30]

Antioch of Pisidia is a kind of crossroads. The Via Sebaste continues westward and is the route that leads to Ephesus. South would take them to Pamphylia, on the southern coast of Asia Minor, where they had evangelized on Paul's First Missionary Journey. The road north would take them through the Province of Asia towards the Roman province of Bythinia and Pontus. But as they consider which way to go – or perhaps have even started on the western road towards Ephesus – God stops them.

> "… Having been kept by the Holy Spirit from preaching the word in the province of Asia." (Acts 16:6, NIV)

The verb "kept" can denote "to forbid" (NRSV, ESV, KJV) or to "prevent."[31] This could have been a prophecy they received while at the church in Lystra or Iconium. Or a personal word to Paul or Silas. Notice that it doesn't come with much content or explanation, except, "No." Much later in their Second Missionary Journey, they have a long and fruitful ministry in Ephesus (Acts 19), but now isn't the time. God has other plans for them – and they are sensitive to the Holy Spirit's nudges.

Don't preach in Bithynia (Acts 16:7-8). So they travel the road north from Antioch of Pisidia that will eventually lead to the Roman Province of Bithynia/Pontus, and the great cities of Nicea, Nicomedia, and Chalcedon along the Black Sea. The apostles' road winds through the Province of Asia – so instead of evangelizing along the way, they continue without stopping to preach, since they've been forbidden to preach in Asia. Finally, they reach Mysia, a region in the north of the Province of Asia. They haven't been forbidden to preach in the Province of Bithynia/Pontus, so they make ready to cross the border – and again the Holy Spirit stops them.

---

[30] The eastern end of the Via Sebaste began in Derbe, then it passed through Lystra, Iconium, Pisidian Antioch, and continued west, almost to the Meander River valley, along which they would then travel to pass through Colossae and Laodicea, and finally cross over to Ephesus.

[31] "Kept" (NIV), "forbidden" (NRSV, ESV, KJV) is the Aorist tense of *kōlyō* followed by an infinitive, "forbid or prevent someone to do or from doing something" (BDAG 580, 1).

"7 When they came to the border of Mysia, they tried to enter Bithynia, but the Spirit of Jesus **would not allow** them to. 8 So they passed by Mysia and went down to Troas." (Acts 16:7-8)

The Greek verb has the force of "prevent, not permit, not allow."[32] Paul and his party receive a clear "No." They can't evangelize in the Roman Provinces of Asia and Bithynia/Pontus. So they turn west towards Troas – a port city on the Aegean Sea. (Troas itself still in the Province of Asia). They're probably very frustrated – maybe grumbling – yet still obedient. God, what are we supposed to *do*?

The Macedonian Vision (Acts 16:9-10). They spend the night in Troas. Finally, their direction comes.

"9 During the night Paul had a vision of a man of Macedonia standing and begging him, 'Come over to Macedonia and help us.' 10 After Paul had seen the vision, we got ready at once to leave for Macedonia, concluding that God had called us to preach the gospel to them." (Acts 16:9-10)

Paul has a dream – or vision – or whatever. In it, a Macedonian begs him to come to Macedonia and help them. Paul, who has had years of experience following the Lord's direction, draws the conclusion that this is indeed a call from God.[33] They sail for Macedonia and have powerful ministries in the Macedonian cities of Philippi, Thessalonica, and Berea.

We learn several things from this string of incidents.

1. **God doesn't always tell us where we are going.** We are expected to follow Jesus, rather than head for the "objective." So their missionary objective is revealed progressively, partly through "noes."

2. **We are to keep going with the guidance we seem to have**, even though our objective isn't clear. God doesn't give us examples of his servants sitting down in the middle of the road, refusing to move until God speaks to them. They keep going.

---

[32] The words "not allow" (NIV, NRSV, ESV), "suffered them not" (KJV) are the negative particle *ou* plus the Aorist tense of the verb *eaō*, "to allow someone to do something, let, permit," with the negative, "prevent, not permit" (BDAG 269, 1).

[33] "Concluding" (NIV, ESV), "being convinced" (NRSV), "assuredly gathering" (KJV) is *symbibazō*, from "to cause to coalesce, to join together, put together," then by extension, "to put together in one's mind, to compare; by comparison, to gather, conclude, consider"(Thayer, *Greek Lexicon*, 595, 2), here, "to draw a conclusion in the face of evidence, conclude, infer" (BDAG 956, 2).

3. **God's guidance is sometimes a "no," rather than a clear positive word.** I think of this as prompting, a nudge – go this way, or don't go that way. As we begin to listen for God's guidance, these nudges become clearer.

Province of Asia: "No."
Province of Bythinia/Pontus: "No."
Macedonia: "Come over and help us!"

Q1. (Acts 8:26-40; 16:6-10) Are promptings from the Holy Spirit clear enough when we're seeking God for direction? Why is "no" just as important an answer as "yes"? Have you ever felt God's promptings to take some action? If you followed through, what happened?
http://www.joyfulheart.com/forums/topic/1771-q1-promptings/

David Inquiring of the Lord (1 and 2 Samuel)

We can see this idea of short, inarticulate directions in David's inquiring of the Lord. After Saul openly seeks to kill him, David lives with a band of men, always on the run. When Saul slaughters the priests because he believes them sympathetic to David, one escapes and comes to David, one hunted man taking refuge with another.

"When Abiathar the son of Ahimelech had fled to David to Keilah, he had come down with an ephod in his hand." (1 Samuel 23:6)

This ephod was presumably part of the high priest's garments, to which was attached a breastplate pouch containing the Urim and the Thummim (Exodus 28, especially vs. 30; cf. Leviticus 8:8). These were apparently sacred lots used by the priests to determine the will of God.[34] They could give a positive answer, a negative answer, and occasionally, no answer at all. If Urim and Thummim were two marked stones that were cast, an answer of "yes" might be both up, a "no" both down, and "no answer" one up and one down. But this is speculation on my part; we're not actually told.

David would pose a question and wait for an answer.

---

[34] You can see the research behind this in my article, "Inquiring of the Lord" (www.joyfulheart.com/scholar/inquire.htm).

"David inquired of the LORD, 'Shall I go and attack the Philistines? Will you hand them over to me?' The LORD answered him, 'Go, for I will surely hand the Philistines over to you.'" (2 Samuel 5:19)

Though this sounds almost like a prophetic word, it is explained adequately as a "yes" answer given by the Urim and Thummim. You see this sort of yes-no answer several times:

- Whether to rescue the town of Keilah from the Philistines (1 Samuel 23:2-4).
- Whether the residents of Keilah will betray David to Saul (1 Samuel 23:9-12).
- Which town to take refuge in (2 Samuel 2:1). The answer is "Hebron," but this can be explained as an answer by lot, just as the determination by lot that wrong lay with Achan (Joshua 7:16-18) or Jonathan (1 Samuel 14:41-42).
- Whether to pursue the Amalekites after their attack on Ziklag (1 Samuel 30:7-8).
- Whether to attack the Philistines at the Valley of Rephaim on the first occasion (2 Samuel 5:19).

But when the Philistines attack a second time and gather at the Valley of Rephaim, the answer David receives goes much beyond a "yes" or "no" that could be obtained from the Urim and Thummim. Rather it is full battle plan, a clear word – either prophecy through Abiathar the priest or a clear word to David himself, who had prophetic gifts abundantly displayed in the Psalms.

"And the Philistines came up yet again and spread out in the Valley of Rephaim. And when David inquired of the LORD, he said, 'You shall not go up; go around to their rear, and come against them opposite the balsam trees. And when you hear the sound of marching in the tops of the balsam trees, then rouse yourself, for then the LORD has gone out before you to strike down the army of the Philistines.' And David did as the LORD commanded him, and struck down the Philistines from Geba to Gezer." (2 Samuel 5:22-25)

This is a great example of "yes" and "no" nudges combined occasionally with clear sentences of revelation from God.

Q2. (2 Samuel 5:19, 22-25) What's the similarity between God's brief, inarticulate nudges or promptings, and David's use of the Urim and Thummim to receive direction? What happens when David needs more than a "yes" or "no" answer? http://www.joyfulheart.com/forums/topic/1772-q2-urim-and-thummim/

Supernatural Spiritual Insight

Here's another incident of a Holy Spirit nudge.

"⁸ In Lystra there sat a man crippled in his feet, who was lame from birth and had never walked. ⁹ He listened to Paul as he was speaking. Paul looked directly at him, **saw that he had faith to be healed** ¹⁰ and called out, 'Stand up on your feet!' At that, the man jumped up and began to walk." (Acts 14:8-10)

While preaching, Paul has an insight from the Holy Spirit – that man has faith to be healed. I doubt that the message came in words. Probably it was just a thought that came with great assurance, but it was clearly a Holy Spirit nudge. Paul acted on it and the man was instantly healed.

Is This a 'Word of Knowledge'?

Some people call this a "word of knowledge" (1 Corinthians 12:8), an insight from God that a person wouldn't normally have unless God revealed it. Jesus certainly models the use of supernatural knowledge in ministry when he reveals to the Samaritan woman her five former husbands (John 4:17-18). As a result of her testimony about the man who "told me everything I ever did," many in her city were converted.

Peter experienced this too, knowing the secret sin of Ananias and Sapphira (Acts 5:1-11) and when he rebuked Simon the Sorcerer: "for I see that you are full of bitterness and captive to sin" (Acts 8:23).

This is actually quite common in ministry. John Wimber, founder of the Vineyard churches, used to encourage teams of people praying for the sick to inquire from an individual why he or she came for prayer, and then ask God quietly to show team members how to pray for the person. Often God would show them something as an image or a single word or two – a nudge rather than a full blown sentence. But often that's enough. Then these insights would guide what was often direct and powerful ministry to the individual.

At one point in my ministry I could "see" from the pulpit the people who were coming under conviction. Maybe I was getting good at "reading my audience," but I believe it was more than that. Many pastors I know seek God diligently for what they should preach on – and find God's clear direction for their congregation. Often the guidance comes in nudges and noes as we seek to find God's word for the hour.

Seeking Direction in Regular Prayer

I pray daily for the people in my life to whom I am close, or have responsibility for – family members and relatives, church leaders, men in my discipleship groups, government leaders, etc. Sometimes when I am praying, God will use the opportunity to nudge me towards a particular person's need.

For example, when I was praying for the spiritual life of an older relative, God guided me to subscribe her to a monthly devotional guide, which she continues to ask me to renew.

As I was praying for a sister-in-law, God prompted me to talk to her about her devotional life when we met at a family gathering. When I brought it up, she seemed quite open, so I suggested regular Bible reading. "Do you have a Bible," I asked. "Somewhere," she said, but it turned out it wasn't in an easy-to-read translation. God brought to my mind a New Testament I had purchased for a couple I was counseling, but hadn't given them. God nudged me to give it to my sister-in-law. "Oh, good," she said. "Large print." God knew she would need large print, I didn't. When I talked with her later, she was still reading the Bible regularly. God is good.

My pastor makes Starbucks coffee shops his functional office. In the course of a day he will meet people there for appointments, but also see many people whom he knows. He prays constantly, "God, how can I engage this person in a conversation about you?" Then he is alert for the openings God provides. Last week he saw a lady he knew while shopping in the grocery store. God prompted him to wait outside until she had finished her shopping, then speak with her. It turned out to be a significant ten-minute conversation!

> Q3. (Acts 5:1-11; 8:23; 14:8-10) Sometimes God nudges you by giving you insight into the spiritual state of people around you. What should you be asking God about once you receive this insight about them? Have you ever had a nudge from God that resulted in a person receiving help? What did you learn from this?
> http://www.joyfulheart.com/forums/topic/1773-q3-nudges-and-insights/

Everyday Nudges

As you develop a conversational relationship with God, you'll find that his nudges don't have to be about "spiritual" things only, but about the needs of everyday life.

Recently, my daughter and son-in-law had purchased their first house, and were getting it ready to move into it. But there was much to do, and they had to move out of their apartment in less than a week. God woke me up about 4 am with the conviction that they needed to get professional help for the flooring installation. When they came to drop off the kids, they agreed and asked me to find an installer. In California, we're in the midst of a building boom, with few tradesmen quickly available. The first installer I called, told me he could begin the following Tuesday. Other installers I phoned said they were backed up with work for three weeks. When I called back, the first installer found he could begin earlier. He and his helper worked Monday and Tuesday and did a great job. Wednesday through Friday, relatives helped with painting, and my daughter and her family were able to move in on Saturday. This may not sound like much, but it is clear to me that God intervened to help my daughter's family get moved in time. God is good.

Where Have You Seen God Lately?

Part of the problem we have is that most of us are not sensitized to recognizing what God is doing around us. In order to bring about this sensitivity, our pastor regularly instructs people during the Sunday morning "greeting" time to ask their neighbor, "Where have you seen God lately?" It can be an awkward question if you haven't seen God at work lately. But gradually you begin to look for places where God showed up. Jesus told the Pharisees, who wanted to stop Sabbath healings.

> "My Father is always at his work to this very day, and I, too, am working." (John 5:17)

Assuming that God is constantly working all around us, we should expect to see God often, once we know what to look for.

When you are looking to buy a house, you see rooms and views and possibilities. But if you bring in a professional home inspector, he sees problems – water stains, weaknesses, circuit malfunctions, plumbing problems, potential roof leaks, etc. He has trained eyes. In the same way, the average citizen walking through a neighborhood will see a lot less than a police officer who knows the community from constant observation.

My brother, my sister, you and I need our eyes trained to see how God is working and our ears tuned to hear his whispers and nudges. Remember Jesus' words:

> "I tell you the truth, the Son can do nothing by himself; he can do only what he sees his Father doing, because whatever the Father does the Son also does. For the

Father loves the Son and shows him all he does. Yes, to your amazement he will show him even greater things than these." (John 5:19-20)

Is God Talking Non-Stop?

A helpful analogy to hearing God's voice is tuning in to a radio station. We don't hear because we're not tuned in.

The problem with this analogy, if you push it, is that many radio stations broadcast 24 hours a day, 7 days a week. God is always at work, but we have no indication in Scripture that he is always talking. We saw earlier in this lesson that as Paul crosses the Province of Asia on his Second Missionary Journey, God isn't saying much – except for an occasional, "No." Paul had to plead three times for God to remove the "thorn in the flesh" before God speaks to him.

The implications are:

1. Don't be discouraged if you don't hear from God. He may not be talking to you right now.
2. We wait on God for his direction; he is not to wait on us or cater to our convenience. We have no right to demand the Sovereign of the Universe to speak to us. We're encouraged to "wait on the Lord" (Psalm 27:14, which we'll examine in Lesson 5). He is not *our* servant to order around; we are *his* humble servants.

Having said this, don't use this as an excuse or cop-out not to listen for his voice. God's voice in words and sentences might be less frequent, but his nudges and promptings can be quite frequent at times.

A housekeeper checks in with her employer frequently to see if there's anything special going on today, but then she continues her regular duties that keep the household running.

We seek God every day and listen for his voice and guidance. Sometimes we hear something and act on it. Other times we don't, but continue in the patterns in which he has led us previously until he indicates that a change is in order. Keep listening. Today may be a special day in his Kingdom for you!

Q4. (Acts 16:6-10; Psalm 27:14) Why does God sometimes *not* talk to us? Is it always because we aren't receptive? What should we do when we don't hear anything from God?
http://www.joyfulheart.com/forums/topic/1774-q4-when-god-is-silent/

God's Nudges to Us Provide Incremental Encouragement to People He Loves

It's important that we get this in perspective. God's promptings don't usually result in earth-shattering, life-altering consequences as we obey them. God has been working incrementally in your life over years and years.

"For it is precept upon precept, precept upon precept,
line upon line, line upon line,
here a little, there a little." (Isaiah 28:10)

It's the same way when you obey God's prompting to say a word to a person or do a kind act. You are God's gentle, incremental encouragement to them. There may not be much dramatic change at any one time, but over time tremendous changes occur.

When I was in Africa, I saw a simple game played by children that involved rolling a tire or hoop. The idea is to keep the hoop upright and rolling by an occasional touch or nudge to alter its direction slightly. I've rolled tires as an adult. You don't have to continually push, since the tire has its own momentum. All you have to do is give an occasional small push or directional nudge.

If you are humble and obedient to God's promptings, you'll find yourself providing this kind of occasional encouragement to the people whom God loves. Listening, obedient servants are what makes God's love real in our world.

Lessons for Disciples

We've considered a number of things as we've explored God's promptings.

1. In addition to messages articulated in clear words and sentences, God often speaks to us in nudges, promptings, inarticulate impressions in the mind to do this or that – or *not* to do something.

2. An example of a nudge is Philip the Evangelist as he encounters the Ethiopian eunuch with two promptings: (a) Gaza road, and (b) chariot (Acts 8:26-40).

3. On his second missionary journey God tells Paul "no" to preaching in the Province of Asia, and "no" to preaching in Bythinia. Only in Troas does he receive a vision of the Macedonian who invites him to Macedonia (Acts 16:6-10).

4. David inquires of God by means of the Urim and Thummim (1 Samuel 23:6; Exodus 28:30; Leviticus 8:8), which gave yes and no answers (e.g., 2 Samuel 5:19), but he also received complex revelations from God when necessary (2 Samuel 5:22-25).

5. Peter and Paul receive insights about the spiritual state of people they were dealing with (Acts 5:1-11; 8:23; 14:8-10). This might be similar to a word of knowledge.

6. God can give nudges about spiritual matters as well as everyday needs of our lives and the lives of others.

7. The question, "Where have you seen God lately?" is helpful to train us to discern what God is doing around us.

8. The Bible doesn't indicate that God talks to us non-stop, if we were only tuned in. So we shouldn't be discouraged if we don't hear from God immediately. Rather we should "wait on the Lord" (Psalm 27:14) as his humble servants.

9. God uses us to provide incremental encouragements to people under God's direction, not usually life-changing words from God.

Week 3 Assignment. Sensitize Yourself: Where Have You Seen God Lately?

As I mentioned above, at Rock Harbor Covenant Church where I attend, a common question we're encouraged to ask one another is, "Where have you seen God lately?"

It's sometimes an embarrassing question. Long silences ensue. But the purpose of the question is to train us to recognize God at work around us – in the little things as well as the occasional big things.

God is constantly at work. He doesn't stop for rest days (John 5:17). Our problem is that our eyes aren't trained to see him at work. What we see, we attribute exclusively to human causation. If we're to discern God's voice, this has to change. We have to become sensitive to him working all around us. Jesus said,

> "I tell you the truth, the Son can do nothing by himself; he can do only what he sees his Father doing, because whatever the Father does the Son also does." (John 5:19)

Learning to discern God at work is foundational to training yourself to hear his voice and pick up on his whispers, promptings, and nudges. Your assignment this week is to talk with your spiritual partner every day, and ask the question, "Where have you seen God working today?" Then explain where you have seen God at work that day.

Prayer

Lord, thank you for your patience to lead us with whispers, promptings, and nudges. And sometimes, "No." Help us to be listening continually, and quickly responsive so you can trust us with more assignments in your Kingdom. Thank you for caring enough to include us in your work. In Jesus' name, we pray. Amen.

Key Verses

"Now an angel of the Lord said to Philip, "Go south to the road – the desert road – that goes down from Jerusalem to Gaza.'" (Acts 8:26, NIV)

"The Spirit told Philip, 'Go to that chariot and stay near it.'" (Acts 8:29, NIV)

"Paul and his companions traveled throughout the region of Phrygia and Galatia, having been kept by the Holy Spirit from preaching the word in the province of Asia. When they came to the border of Mysia, they tried to enter Bithynia, but the Spirit of Jesus would not allow them to. So they passed by Mysia and went down to Troas. During the night Paul had a vision of a man of Macedonia standing and begging him, "Come over to Macedonia and help us." After Paul had seen the vision, we got ready at once to leave for Macedonia, concluding that God had called us to preach the gospel to them." (Acts 16:6-10, NIV)

"When Abiathar the son of Ahimelech had fled to David to Keilah, he had come down with an ephod in his hand." (1 Samuel 23:6, NIV)

"David inquired of the LORD, 'Shall I go and attack the Philistines? Will you hand them over to me?' The LORD answered him, 'Go, for I will surely hand the Philistines over to you.'" (2 Samuel 5:19, NIV)

"In Lystra there sat a man crippled in his feet, who was lame from birth and had never walked. He listened to Paul as he was speaking. Paul looked directly at him, saw that he had faith to be healed and called out, 'Stand up on your feet!' At that, the man jumped up and began to walk." (Acts 14:8-10, NIV)

"My Father is always at his work to this very day, and I, too, am working." (John 5:17, NIV)

4. Heart Preparation for Listening to God (1 Samuel 3:1-10)

If you're not used to it, listening for and hearing God's leading can seem overwhelming. In this lesson we'll consider how you can prepare yourself to listen, with some simple guidelines that will help you be more receptive to God's whispers.

Samuel: "Speak Lord, for your servant is listening" (1 Samuel 3:1-10)

We begin with the story of Samuel hearing God's voice for the first time in the temple. As you recall, Hannah who had been barren, is given a child.

Edward Burne-Jones, detail of 'Samuel' (1873), Vyning Memorial Windows, Christ Cathedral, Oxford.

> "So in the course of time Hannah conceived and gave birth to a son. She named him Samuel, saying, Because I asked the LORD for him.'" (1 Samuel 1:20)

The name Samuel (*shemû'ēl*) sounds like the Hebrew for "heard of God," *shāma'*, "hear, listen to" and *'ēl*, the generic word for "God."

Little Samuel is dedicated to the Lord, and after Hannah weans him, he lives at the tabernacle (sometimes called "the temple" or sanctuary) at Shiloh under the care of Eli the priest. Every year his mother brings him a new ephod to wear.

He seems to be sleeping in the temple itself when he is awakened by the sound of his name being called. He runs to Eli, who says he didn't call him and sends him back to bed. It happens again with the same result. Then the writer tells us:

> "7 Now Samuel did not yet know the LORD: The word (*dābār*) of the LORD had not yet been revealed to him.
>
> 8 The LORD called Samuel a third time, and Samuel got up and went to Eli and said, 'Here I am; you called me.' Then Eli realized that the LORD was calling the

boy. [9] So Eli told Samuel, 'Go and lie down, and if he calls you, say, "Speak, LORD, for your servant is listening."'

So Samuel went and lay down in his place. [10] The LORD came and stood there, calling as at the other times, 'Samuel! Samuel!'

Then Samuel said, 'Speak, for your servant is listening.'" (1 Samuel 3:7-10)

Eli is correct in discerning that Yahweh is calling the boy, and his instruction of what to say is right on target:

"Speak, LORD, for your servant is listening." (verse 9b)

"Speak" is the Piel imperative of the common Hebrew verb *dābar*, "to speak."[35]

"LORD" in caps designates God's specific name, Yahweh.

"Servant" is *'ebed*, "servant, slave." The term is used as a polite and humble way to refer to oneself (Genesis 33:5; 2 Kings 8:13). In the case of a king, all his subjects are considered his servants, including all who serve him directly – his officers, officials, and ambassadors. The expression "your servant" is frequently used when addressing God in prayer.[36]

"Is listening" (NIV, NRSV), **"hears"** (ESV), "heareth" (KJV) is the Qal participle of *shāma'*, which, you remember, is the word from which Samuel's name is formed. *Shāma'* has the basic meaning "to hear." This is extended in various ways, generally involving an *effective* hearing or listening, "hear, listen to, obey."[37] Samuel places himself in the position of a servant whose master has called him, so he comes ready to listen to his master's command, and then obediently carry out his command.

Once Samuel has answered in this way, Yahweh tells this young child of the awesome judgment that He will bring against Eli and his sons for their terrible sins, a message that Yahweh has previously spoken to Eli through "a man of God" (1 Samuel 2:27-36).

In the morning, when Eli asks Samuel what Yahweh has told him, Samuel is too frightened to say. But when Eli threatens him, he spills out the prophecy. When he has finished, Eli confirms that Samuel has heard correctly:

"It is the LORD. Let him do what seems good to him." (1 Samuel 3:18)

---

[35] *Dābar*, TWOT #399. The word has a wide range of meaning, from "declare" to "command," from "promise" to "threaten," and all in between. From the verb *dābar*, "speak," comes the noun *dābār*, "word," found in verse 10.

[36] Walter C. Kaiser, *'ebed*, TWOT #1553a.

[37] *Shāma'*, TWOT #2412.

Eli recognizes Yahweh's message all too well. He hadn't responded with repentance the first time he heard it, nor does he do so now.

What We Can Learn from Samuel's Call

The story teaches us several things:

1. You can worship but not know God, at least not know him intimately. Verse 10 tells us: "Now Samuel did not yet know the LORD: The word of the LORD had not yet been revealed to him." Samuel has been worshipping[38] Yahweh in the sanctuary (1 Samuel 1:28b) and ministering[39] before Yahweh (1 Samuel 3:1) – that is, assisting in the priestly duties – without knowing God!

2. You can hear God speaking, but not recognize that it is God. We may not recognize God's voice the first time we hear it. It wouldn't surprise me if you who are reading this have heard God speaking to you, but haven't recognized it as God himself speaking. Perhaps you identified it as your conscience or your own thoughts.

3. Sometimes a mentor can help us learn to recognize and respond to God's voice. Eli recognizes what is happening and instructs Samuel on what to say if this happens again (1 Samuel 3:9). Then the mentor confirms that it is indeed God's voice that Samuel heard – "It is the LORD" (1 Samuel 3:18) – though Samuel is already well aware that God has spoken to him. We'll talk more about mentors in Lesson 5.

4. We must come before God as humble and obedient servants if we want to hear what he is saying. It is quite possible to hear without listening. In each of the four Gospels, Jesus quotes Isaiah to explain his reason for teaching in parables:

> "'Be ever hearing, but never understanding;
> be ever seeing, but never perceiving.'
> Make the heart of this people calloused;
> make their ears dull and close their eyes.
> Otherwise they might see with their eyes,
> hear with their ears,

---

[38] "Worshipped" is now understood to be the Eshtaphal stem of *ḥāwā*. (Edwin Yamauchi, *shāḥā*, TWOT #2360). "The commonly occurring form *hishtaḥăwâ*, 'to prostrate oneself' or 'to worship,' which was analyzed as a Hithpael of *shāḥā*, is now regarded on the basis of Ugaritic evidence as an *Eshtaphal* stem (the only example) of *ḥāwā* (Edwin Yamauchi, TWOT #619). Holladay sees this as an Histafal stem (pp. 97a, 365b).

[39] "Ministered" is the Piel stem of *shārat*, "minister, serve," used to describe (1) personal service rendered to an important person or (2) the ministry of worship on the part of those who stand in a special relationship to God, such as the priests (Hermann J. Austel, TWOT #2472).

understand with their hearts,
and turn and be healed." (Isaiah 6:9-10)

As I mentioned before, it's possible for husbands to develop "selective hearing" towards their wives, only tuning in to what they *want* to hear. And so we can be with God.

Q1. (1 Samuel 3:1-10) What was Eli's counsel to Samuel, when he recognized that God was calling to the boy? Was it good counsel? What is the significance of Samuel recognizing that he is a servant?
http://www.joyfulheart.com/forums/topic/1775-q1-listening-servant/

It Is the Relationship, not the Voice, that We Seek

Samuel's story reminds us that for us to hear God, there are some things in us that need adjusting. Earlier we read, "Samuel did not yet know the LORD" (1 Samuel 3:7), speaking of intimate personal relationship.[40] Now he does.

First and foremost, our goal must be knowing God himself, not just experiencing the supposed novelty of hearing his voice. Hearing his voice is not a gimmick or spiritual token to attain so you can brag about it. Hearing his voice is part of a conversational relationship. Indeed, it adds greatly to the receiving part of communication.

As we studied Jesus' prayer life in Lesson 1 it becomes clear that spending time with God enables Jesus to see and hear what the Father was doing, so he can do it also. It maintains his relationship with his Father. Hosea exhorts us:

"**Let us know;**
let us press on to know the LORD;
his going out is sure as the dawn;
he will come to us as the showers,
as the spring rains that water the earth." (Hosea 6:3, ESV)

"Know" (ESV, NRSV, KJV), "acknowledge" (NIV) is *yāda* ', "know," with many shades of knowledge, from intimate sexual knowledge (Genesis 4:1), to 'discern,' as well as the most intimate acquaintance, such as Moses, whom Yahweh knows "face-to-face" (Deuteronomy 34:10).[41] Hosea calls on us to "**press on** to know the Lord." The verb is *rādap*, "be

---

[40] Paul R. Gilchrist, *yāda* ', TWOT #848.
[41] Paul R. Gilchrist, *yāda* ', TWOT #848.

behind, follow after, pursue"[42] We are to chase after God, pursue him, so that we might know him well. You can sense Paul's passion to know Christ better:

> "**I want to know Christ**.... I **press on** to take hold of that for which Christ Jesus took hold of me.... Forgetting what is behind and **straining toward** what is ahead, I **press on** toward the goal to win the prize for which God has called me heaven-ward in Christ Jesus." (Philippians 3:10-14)

The Greek for "press on" in Philippians 3 has a similar idea to that of the Hebrew, "to move rapidly and decisively toward an objective, hasten, run, press on ... to follow in haste in order to find something, run after, pursue."[43]

A.W. Tozer wrote a powerful book, *The Pursuit of God* (1948), still valuable today for those passionate to know Him. Tozer cites a wide variety of Christian leaders, and then asks, What vital quality ties them together?

> "I venture to suggest that the one vital quality which they had in common was **spiritual receptivity**. Something in them was open to heaven, something which urged them Godward.... They had spiritual awareness and ... **they went on to cultivate it until it became the biggest thing in their lives**. They differed from the average person in that when they felt the inward longing they did something about it. They acquired the lifelong habit of spiritual response.... **Receptivity is ... an affinity for, a bent toward, a sympathetic response to, a desire to have.**"[44]

David, a man after God's own heart (Acts 13:22), wrote,

> "You have said, 'Seek my face.'
> My heart says to you,
> 'Your face, LORD, do I seek.'" (Psalm 27:8)

Developing a relationship with God comes before seeking to hear God's voice, because a relationship is based on trust. And trusting God is necessary or we won't follow through with the hard things God will be asking us to do.

When Jesus moves beyond feeding multitudes with bread, and speaks of people eating his own flesh and drinking his blood, "many of his disciples turned back and no longer followed him." Those who stayed, remained because of a relationship, a receptivity to Jesus. "Lord, to whom shall we go? You have the words of eternal life" (John 6:66-68).

---

[42] *Rādap*, TWOT #2124.
[43] *Diōkō*, BDAG 254, 1 and 4.
[44] A.W. Tozer, *The Pursuit of God* (1948), chapter 5.

Hearing God's voice flows out of a relationship. It is wed to our life of prayer before God.

Q2. (1 Samuel 3:7; Hosea 6:3; Philippians 3:10-14) Why is a desire for a relationship with God more important than seeking to hear his voice? How does hearing his voice contribute to the relationship? Why are we commanded to "press in" to know the Lord? How does Paul's passion for a relationship with God inspire you? http://www.joyfulheart.com/forums/topic/1776-q2-to-know-god/

Learning to Follow Orders without Questioning

We learn from Samuel, that a willingness to obey is an important part of being receptive to God's voice: "Speak, LORD, for **your servant** hears." A servant hears with the intention of obeying what his master tells him. It is insulting to ask God what we should do if we have no intention of doing anything else than what *we* want to do.

Part of a willing and submissive spirit is a willingness to obey:
1. Even if we don't understand why, and
2. Even if we don't know the final result.

Too often there is in us an insistence on being in control. Explain it to me, God, and if I agree that it fits my objectives and plans for my life, then I'll be happy to obey. How silly! In the military, the importance of following orders is drilled into soldiers – and officers. Alfred Lord Tennyson's poem "Charge of the Light Brigade" (1854) contains the immortal words:

> "Theirs not to make reply,
> Theirs not to reason why,
> Theirs but to do and die."

In war, if the lowliest private demands to know all the details of the strategy before he or she obeys orders, then the unit loses its ability to move quickly as one.

Only if a soldier receives what is an illegal order or command should he or she refuse. In the same way, when we become familiar with the Bible, we know the kinds of commands that God would never give, and thus discern that it is not God's voice telling us that. More on discerning God's voice in Lesson 5.

Jonah is an example of a person who hasn't surrendered himself to God. He hates the compassion and mercy that God stands for, so when God commands him to prophesy to his nation's enemies at Nineveh, the capital of Assyria, he rebels against God, going the opposite direction. Even after God uses him to bring a revival and repentance to Nineveh, he is selfish and petulant. Finally, God sets him in his place, by saying, "Do you have a right to be angry, Jonah." It isn't your plant, it's mine. Nineveh isn't your people to decide their fate, they are mine and they don't have a clue spiritually.

God Leads by Seeing the Whole Picture (Psalm 32:8-9)

God sees the whole picture, as a reconnaissance pilot who watches the battle from a spotter plane high above the action, and radios down the instructions for battle. God speaks through David in Psalm 32:

> "I will instruct you and teach you in the way you should go;
> I will counsel you with my eye upon you.
> Be not like a horse or a mule, without understanding,
> which must be curbed with bit and bridle,
> or it will not stay near you." (Psalm 32:8-9, ESV)

God is our instructor and teacher on what way or path to take. From his vantage point – seeing the past, present, and future – God sees what we cannot see, and "counsels us with his eye upon us."[45] If we will listen, God is our wise counselor.

Notice that God doesn't want to force us to obey – like some animals that won't obey unless you put a bit and bridle on them. Rather he seeks to speak to us in counsel. As we have faith in him, we begin to obey. He desires a more mature relationship based on trust rather than force. If we fight him, we can't serve him.

We'll Only Know When We're Willing to Trust

There's a sense that only when we *do* obey what God shows us will we find out what he is planning to do through us. When we resist, we'll never know. When faced with the his enemies' unbelief, Jesus said:

> "If anyone chooses to do God's will,
> he will find out whether my teaching comes from God
> or whether I speak on my own." (John 7:17)

As an old folk proverb puts it, "The proof of the pudding is in the eating." You'll never know what God is doing unless you obey. Even then you may not know how your small act of obedience fits into his larger plan. But occasionally you'll be able to see the fruit,

---

[45] "Counsel" (NIV, NRSV, ESV), "guide" (KJV) is *yāʿas*, "advise, counsel" (TWOT #887).

and can rejoice. I only wonder what other things I could have rejoiced about if I had only listened and obeyed always.

> Q3. (Psalm 32:8-9; John 7:17) Why is a willingness to obey without understanding the reasons for God's commands so important? How does obedience sometimes help us understand God's workings.
> http://www.joyfulheart.com/forums/topic/1777-q3-willing-to-obey/

Waiting on the Lord (Psalm 27:14)

The desire for control keeps us from humble submission to God. We don't *have* to know everything.

In Lesson 2 we studied Paul's reaction to the "thorn in the flesh." He pleads with God three times to remove it. God doesn't answer his prayer. But God's reply gives a hint of *why* he didn't answer Paul's prayer. He is teaching Paul the strength that comes with full dependence upon God.

In Lesson 3 we examined the series of frustrating "noes" from God as Paul and his party travel across Asia Minor, seeking God's leading about where to evangelize (Acts 16:6-10). God only speaks to them after weeks of travel – and then in a dream. God is fully able to speak to you. Don't try to force him to speak. He'll speak in his good time. That's part of being a submissive servant – the place that Samuel assumed before God. "Speak, Lord, for your servant is listening" (1 Samuel 3:9-10)

This is what it means to "wait on the Lord."

> "Wait for the LORD;
> be strong,
> and let your heart take courage;
> wait for the LORD!" (Psalm 27:14, ESV)

"Wait" is *qāwâ*, "to wait or to look for with eager expectation."[46] I ran across something from Lynette Haigen that describes this kind of submissive waiting on God that is part of servant obedience. We pick it up where she asks God about a particular situation.

---

[46] John E. Hartley, *qāwâ*, TWOT #1994. In Psalm 24:14, the Piel imperative of *qāwâ* appears twice. See also Psalm 33:20; 130:5; Isaiah 8:17; Habakkuk 2:3; Luke 2:25; Romans 8:25.

"… Then I rest in peace. I may not have direction at the moment, but I am confident that the answer will come. I do not worry or fret about it. When I am tempted to be anxious or concerned, I simply remind the Lord that I need an answer.

That answer may come days, weeks, or even months later. I may be worshipping and praising the Lord when suddenly, out of my spirit will come thoughts that are the answer to what I have asked Him. At that moment I may not be thinking about the request. Therefore, I know that these are not my thoughts but the thoughts of the Lord. He is enlightening my spirit and giving me the wisdom I asked Him for."[47]

The Subtlety of Pride

We've already considered the importance of an attitude of a servant vs. our natural desire to control outcomes. Now we need to consider another motivation that we must deliberately avoid when listening for the voice of God – pride. It is subtle, but it is often lurking to contaminate our motives.

When you say confidently, "God told me to ….," people are often impressed. Since they haven't heard from God and we have, it tends to elevate us in their eyes. Woe to us humans, who often walk before God with mixed motives! Forgive us, Lord! I'm not saying that leaders shouldn't declare what God has told them as they lead the people God has put in their charge. But:

1. Don't publicly claim God's guidance unless it is clear.
2. Don't say, "God told me," unless he has really spoken.
3. When you talk about God's guidance, do it with humility. It is God you are trying to promote, not the servant whose ears got cleaned out enough to hear Him.

Remember Simon the Sorcerer, who wanted to purchase the power to confer the Holy Spirit so he could retain control over people (Acts 8:9-25). Peter's retort should caution us:

"You have no part or share in this ministry, because your heart is not right before God. Repent of this wickedness and pray to the Lord. Perhaps he will forgive you for having such a thought in your heart." (Acts 8:21-22)

---

[47] Lynette Haigen, "Hearing God's Voice." Lynette is the wife of Pentecostal teacher Ken Haigen. This was found on the Kenneth Haigen Ministries website. www.rhema.org/index.php?option=com_content&view=article&id=1882

Q4. How can pride corrupt our hearing from God? How do we protect ourselves from being deceived by our pride?
http://www.joyfulheart.com/forums/topic/1778-q4-pride-corrupts/

Lessons for Disciples

We've talked quite a bit about heart preparation and pure motives so that we can hear God well.

1. You can worship but not know God, at least not know him intimately (1 Samuel 3:7)
2. You can hear God speaking, but not recognize that it is God (1 Samuel 3:4-6)
3. Sometimes a mentor can help us learn to recognize and respond to God's voice (1 Samuel 3:9). The mentor might then confirm that it is indeed God's voice that we heard (1 Samuel 3:18).
4. We must come before God as humble and obedient servants if we want to hear what he is saying (1 Samuel 3:9-10).
5. It is the relationship with God, not his voice, that is primary. We are seeking to know him intimately! (Hosea 6:3; Philippians 3:10-14; Psalm 27:8).
6. We need to cultivate spiritual receptivity, an affinity for, a bent toward, a sympathetic response to, a desire to have … God (A.W. Tozer).
7. We must be willing to obey God quickly, without demanding to understand why – as soldiers who serve in an army under the direction of the general who sees the whole picture (Psalm 32:8-9).
8. We'll only know God's will when we're willing to follow him in trust (John 7:17).
9. Waiting for the Lord means that we trust him without demanding that he do something for us now! (Psalm 27:14).
10. We must beware of being filled with pride because God has spoken to us; humility is much more appropriate.

Week 4 Assignment. Ask God Questions and Listen for His Response

You may have started doing this already, but if not, after you have quieted your spirit before him, begin to ask God questions about what's going on in your life. Then be silent and listen to see what God might say to you.

You may receive some distinct impressions, thoughts he may put in your mind – or not. When you feel God is saying something to you, write it down in your journal. Just the act of writing down what you think God might be saying will help clarify it for you. Then ask him about what you think you're hearing. Perhaps you'll hear more. This is a conversation.

You won't always hear God say something. That's okay. Don't try to force God to speak to you or to answer you! He is the sovereign God, not you. Content yourself to be humbly silent in his presence where you can find your spirit renewed.

Nevertheless, you may find him putting thoughts in your mind. If so, praise God. That's a good start.

Your assignment this week is – every day in your Quiet Time – to ask God questions and then be still and listen. If he puts something in your mind write it down. Then share this with your spiritual partner, who may be able to help you discern if this is, indeed, God. Eventually you'll learn to discern God's voice on your own. But in the beginning, feedback from a sympathetic friend is helpful and encouraging.

Prayer

Father, please teach me to seek obedience and trust along with my desire to hear you. Make my heart pure so I can be a servant in whom you are pleased. In Jesus' name, I pray. Amen.

Key Verses

"Now Samuel did not yet know the LORD: The word (*dābār*) of the LORD had not yet been revealed to him.

The LORD called Samuel a third time, and Samuel got up and went to Eli and said, 'Here I am; you called me.' Then Eli realized that the LORD was calling the boy. So Eli told Samuel, 'Go and lie down, and if he calls you, say, "Speak, LORD, for your servant is listening."'

So Samuel went and lay down in his place. The LORD came and stood there, calling as at the other times, 'Samuel! Samuel!'

Then Samuel said, 'Speak, for your servant is listening.'" (1 Samuel 3:7-10, NIV)

"Let us know;
let us press on to know the LORD;
his going out is sure as the dawn;

he will come to us as the showers,
as the spring rains that water the earth." (Hosea 6:3, ESV)

"I want to know Christ…. I press on to take hold of that for which Christ Jesus took hold of me…. Forgetting what is behind and straining toward what is ahead, I press on toward the goal to win the prize for which God has called me heavenward in Christ Jesus." (Philippians 3:10-14, NIV)

"You have said, 'Seek my face.'
My heart says to you,
'Your face, LORD, do I seek.'" (Psalm 27:8, NIV)

"I will instruct you and teach you in the way you should go;
I will counsel you with my eye upon you.
Be not like a horse or a mule, without understanding,
which must be curbed with bit and bridle,
or it will not stay near you." (Psalm 32:8-9, ESV)

"If anyone chooses to do God's will,
he will find out whether my teaching comes from God
or whether I speak on my own." (John 7:17, NIV)

"Wait for the LORD;
be strong,
and let your heart take courage;
wait for the LORD!" (Psalm 27:14, ESV)

5. Discerning God's Voice (Judges 6:36-40)

We've considered how God's words and nudges guided men and women in Bible days. And we've examined the importance of humility, obedience, and an active seeking to grow closer to God. Now we come to a question that many have: How do I discern whether God is speaking to me or not.

Yahweh Speaks to Gideon (Judges 6-8)

We begin with Gideon, who famously asks God for confirmation by giving him a sign – two signs, in fact.

Of course, Gideon isn't the first to seek confirmation of God's word. God offers Moses a burning bush, a staff that turns to a snake, and short-lived leprosy to convince him (Exodus 3-4), plus meeting his brother Aaron in the middle of the vast desert (Exodus 4:27).

But Gideon's request for a sign takes on significance in the Christian jargon as "putting

Gideon pointing to the fleece. Illustrated manuscript, German, Hildesheim, about 1170s, Tempera colors, gold leaf, silver leaf, and ink on parchment, 11 1/8 x 7 7/16 in., MS. 64, FOL. 92. Getty Museum.

out a fleece," so it's worth spending some time considering it.

Gideon lives around 1100 BC during the period of the Judges. During this time, the Israelites are being oppressed by nomadic Midianite and Amalekite peoples, who move into Israel during harvest season and confiscate all the recently-harvested crops, then return to their traditional lands. After seven years of this, the Israelites are impoverished – and demoralized, afraid to resist the overwhelming force of their enemies.

One day, as Gideon is threshing wheat in a winepress to try to avoid being seen by the Midianites, Yahweh appears to him as an angel and encourages him:

"Go in the strength you have and save Israel out of Midian's hand. Am I not sending you?" (Judges 6:14)

Gideon demurs. My clan is the weakest of the tribe of Manasseh, and I am the least in my family. But God won't take no for an answer: "I will be with you."

Showing the appropriate hospitality to strangers that is characteristic of Semitic peoples. Gideon prepares a meal for the man. But the food is instantly consumed by fire when the angel touches it with his staff. Gideon is terrified, suddenly realizing that he has seen an angel of God Almighty.

Later that night, Yahweh (apparently not in the form of an angel this time) speaks to him and commands him to tear down the community's altar to Baal, the fertility god, and the Asherah pole, representing the fertility goddess, beside it. Gideon gets some servants and tears them down.

Now the Spirit of God comes upon Gideon and he blows a trumpet calling out his clan and tribe to rise up against the Midianites. Later, when he realizes what he has set in motion, Gideon is afraid. Was this really You speaking to me, God? What if I get it wrong? If so, I'm really in trouble now! So he asks God for a sign as a confirmation.

Gideon Asks for a Sign (Judges 6:36-38)

"[36] Gideon said to God, 'If you will save Israel by my hand as you have promised – [37] look, I will place a wool fleece on the threshing floor. If there is dew only on the fleece and all the ground is dry, then I will know that you will save Israel by my hand, as you said.' [38] And that is what happened. Gideon rose early the next day; he squeezed the fleece and wrung out the dew – a bowlful of water."

[39] Then Gideon said to God, 'Do not be angry with me. Let me make just one more request. Allow me one more test with the fleece. This time make the fleece dry and the ground covered with dew.' [40] That night God did so. Only the fleece was dry; all the ground was covered with dew." (Judges 6:36-40)

God confirms that he is speaking to Gideon, and Gideon and his famous band of 300 soldiers go on to defeat the combined armies of the Midianites and Amalekites, demonstrating that God keeps his promise to Gideon. Let's examine this account of the fleeces.

First, Gideon clarifies the question that he needs an answer to. He wants to make sure he has the message right – that "You will save[48] Israel by my hand as you have promised" (Judges 6:36). Gideon doesn't see himself as the savior. Rather God will save Israel. But Gideon will be the instrument – "by my hand." This is a curious request for confirmation,

---

[48] "Save" (NIV, KJV) or "deliver" (NRSV) is the Hebrew verb *yāsha`*, "save, deliver, give victory, help; be safe; take vengeance, preserve" (John E. Hartley, TWOT #929).

since Gideon acknowledges at the outset that this is what he understands God's promise to be.[49] Gideon just needs to be certain.

We can certainly empathize with Gideon. How often have we felt God's leading, but need assurance again – and yet again. But God is gracious. Gideon has obeyed all of God's commands so far. He is serious about this request; he just needs assurance.

He sets up the test with a fleece – the sheared pelt of wool from a sheep that has come off in a single piece.[50] He places the fleece on dry, flat ground in the evening – a "threshing floor."[51]

Then Gideon retires for the evening to await the dew. May to October are the dry months when no rain falls. But in the evening, the temperature in Palestine drops dramatically. Moist west winds blow inland from the Mediterranean. The cold nights cause condensation of the moisture. The amount varies in different regions, but in Gaza, for example, there is dew 250 nights of the year.[52]

When Gideon gets up in the morning the fleece is sopping wet and he is able to wring a bowlful of water from it, but the ground around the fleece is dry. God has confirmed his inquiry.

Gideon wonders, scientist that he is, if by some fluke the wool fleece just absorbed more water. Now he asks God to do the opposite the following night – the fleece dry and the ground wet.

His request is humble and tentative – though bold at the same time. He addresses God: "Do not be angry with me. Let me make just one more request. Allow me one more test with the fleece" (Judges 6:39a). He pleads for God's indulgence.

He acknowledges that God has reason to be angry with him. After all God has allowed himself to be put to the test once already. Yet God graciously responds with a clear-cut result.

Tempting or Testing God

Gideon is rightly concerned that God might be angry at his second request for a "test." Why should the Almighty God, after all, have to submit to little exercises invented by

---

[49] "Promised" (NIV) or "said" (KJV) in verse 36 is the verb *dābar*, "to speak, declare, converse, command, promise, warn, threaten, sing, etc." (Earl S. Kalland, TWOT #399).

[50] "Fleece" is the Hebrew noun *gizzâ*, from the verb *gāzaz*, "to shear or mow" (Elmer B. Smick, TWOT #336b).

[51] "Threshing floor" (NIV) or "floor" is the Hebrew noun *gōren*, which refers specifically to "threshing floor, threshing place, the place where grain was threshed from the stalk and chaff" (Harold G. Stigers, TWOT #383a).

[52] Jack P. Lewis, *ṭll*, TWOT #807a. A.H. Joy, "Dew," ISBE 1:941.

mere men? The word "test" (NIV, ESV), "prove" (KJV), or "make trial" (NRSV) in Judges 6:39 is the Hebrew verb *nāsâ*, "test, try, prove, tempt, assay, put to the proof, put to the test."[53]

A number of people have gotten in bad trouble by "putting God to the test," most famously by the Israelites who demand that God give them water and food in the desert (Exodus 17:2, 7; also Psalm 78:18, 41). Later God commands them:

> "Do not **test** the LORD your God as you did at Massah." (Deuteronomy 6:16)

> "Today, if you hear his voice,
> do not harden your hearts as you did at Meribah,
> as you did that day at Massah in the desert,
> where your fathers **tested**[54] and **tried**[55] me,
> though they had seen what I did.
> For forty years I was angry with that generation;
> I said, 'They are a people whose hearts go astray,
> and they have not known my ways.'" (Psalm 95:7b-10)

Demanding for a sign, or that God prove himself to us, is equivalent to "putting the Lord to the **test**" (Isaiah 7:10-12).

In the Gospels, Jesus replies to Satan's taunting dares, "It is also written: 'Do not put the Lord your God to the **test**'" (Matthew 4:7). The Pharisees are constantly demanding that Jesus do miraculous signs.

> "The Pharisees came and began to question Jesus. To **test** him, they asked him for a sign from heaven. He sighed deeply and said, 'Why does this generation ask for a miraculous sign? I tell you the truth, no sign will be given to it.'" (Mark 8:11-12)

> "Then some of the Pharisees and teachers of the law said to him, 'Teacher, we want to see a miraculous sign from you.' He answered, 'A wicked and adulterous generation asks for a miraculous sign! But none will be given it except the sign of the prophet Jonah.'" (Matthew 12:38-39)

> "Even after Jesus had done all these miraculous signs in their presence, they still would not believe in him." (John 12:37)

[53] Marvin R. Wilson, *nāsâ*, TWOT #1373.

[54] Piel perfect of *nāsâ*.

[55] Qal perfect of *bāḥan*, "to examine, try, prove." "*Nāsâ* means 'to put to the test, tempt' (in the archaic sense), while *ṣārap* means "to smelt, refine." *Bāḥan* partakes of both of these in that it denotes examining to determine essential qualities, especially integrity" (John N. Oswalt, TWOT #230).

"For Jews demand[56] signs and Greeks seek wisdom…." (1 Corinthians 1:22)

Demanding that God do something, such as provide food and water in the wilderness, is evidence of a sinful, rebellious, unbelieving heart. *Demanding* that Jesus prove himself by doing miraculous signs – when they already don't believe despite having seen amazing things – is evidence of a mocking attitude of unbelief. Such demanding, unbelieving people get in trouble with God.

Humbly Asking for Confirmation

What's the difference between Gideon's fleece tests and "putting God to the test"? The testing of God we see in the Bible are attempts by unbelievers to demand things of God, or to manipulate God into somehow proving himself. Unless you do this, I won't believe!

But Gideon is asking for God to do a minor miracle to help Gideon anchor his full faith in the Lord. Gideon wants to believe. And he has stuck his neck way out by rallying the tribes to war. Gideon's request is in order to establish his faith so that he might lead God's people. Gideon's request is not an unbelieving testing to get God to do miracles or demands for him to meet Gideon's selfish needs.

Now if Gideon were asking God to repeat the fleece test later on, he would be unbelieving. But in this early stage of becoming sure of God's voice, Gideon rightly asks God to confirm what he thinks God has told him. Later, when he recognizes God's voice, Gideon has no trouble obeying God in cutting down the size of his army from 42,000 to 300 (Judges 7:1-7). Just before the battle, God invites Gideon to overhear a dream that encourages him further (Judges 7:9-15). Gideon doesn't demand further confirmation, but God gives it to him unbidden.

I believe that it is okay for us to ask God for confirmation the first time, or first few times, he speaks to us. But I don't recommend *demanding* a particular confirmation, like Gideon did. A lot of people have said on the spur of the moment, "If you do such-and-such, then I'll know you want me to do this." I don't recommend spontaneous tests of God because they are too often selfish manifestations of unbelief.

Rather, ask God to confirm his direction to you in any way He sees fit. God understands that you're just learning. And he is a good Parent, who isn't offended if you ask for help in learning. In this case, it is *faith* asking for confirmation, not *unbelief* demanding God to prove himself.

---

[56] "Demand" (NIV, NRSV, ESV), "require" (KJV) is *aiteō*, "to ask for, with a claim on receipt of an answer, ask, ask for, demand" (BDAG 30).

Q1. ((Judges 6:36-38; Psalm 95:7-10) Does Gideon ask for a sign because of his un-belief? What is the difference between Gideon's seeking confirmation, and "test-ing God" in a way that displeases God? Does God mind if we ask for confirmation? When might God be upset with us for asking for confirmation? http://www.joyfulheart.com/forums/topic/1779-q1-confirming-vs-testing/

The Voices in Our Head

Our problem in needing confirmation is to sort out which voice in our head might be God speaking to us. Here are several possibilities – though there may be more:

- God's voice – the real thing.
- The World – voices of others, peer pressure, worldly standards of success, etc.
- The Flesh – our own desires and thoughts, many of which are selfish.
- The Devil – demonic temptation and misdirection from Satan and his forces.
- The Conscience – our moral sense of right and wrong that we obtain from our upbringing. Sometimes we are hindered by a skewed sense of justice or right-eousness – perhaps an extreme legalism, or perhaps an insensitivity to certain sins. Our conscience is strongly influenced by the culture we grow up in. How-ever, the conscience can be educated by the Word of God as we seek his way.

Discerning the difference when we're getting started can be confusing.

A Learning Process Involves Mistakes

I hope this doesn't scare you to death, but don't be surprised if you make some mis-takes in discerning whether it is God speaking to you. You fell down when you were learning to walk, but you didn't break any bones. In the same way, you learn to discern what is God's voice, and what isn't, by experience.

I can vividly remember thinking something was God's direction, but when I acted on it, it became obvious that God wasn't in it. I was embarrassed! But such mistakes are nec-essary to the process of learning to recognize God's true voice.

I wish there were some sure-fire way that doesn't entail misunderstandings and mis-takes, but that's the way it is. There are ways to *minimize* mistakes, as I'll describe below, but not to avoid them completely. The writer of Hebrews describes the learning process:

"But solid food is for the mature, who by constant use[57] have trained themselves to distinguish good from evil." (Hebrews 5:14)

It *does* get better. We *can* mature in our sensitivity to and discernment of God's voice.

Q2. (Hebrews 5:14) Why will a person have to make mistakes in the process of learning to discern God's voice? If mistakes are part of the process, how can this be of God at all?
http://www.joyfulheart.com/forums/topic/1780-q2-trial-and-error/

The Voices of the World, the Flesh, and the Devil (Ephesians 2:1-3; 1 John 2:15-17)

If you've spent your entire life in rebellion against God, then the world's voice and Satan's voice seem okay. That's what you've been used to. Paul writes:

"[1] As for you, you were dead in your transgressions and sins, [2] in which you used to live when you followed the ways of this world and of the ruler of the kingdom of the air, the spirit who is now at work in those who are disobedient. [3] All of us also lived among them at one time, gratifying the cravings of our sinful nature and following its desires and thoughts. Like the rest, we were by nature objects of wrath." (Ephesians 2:1-3)

By default we followed the ways of Satan, "the ruler of the kingdom of the air," and adopted the standards of morality and behavior held by the world around us, "following its thoughts and desires." But God has shown grace to us. Now we need to unlearn the ways of the world and our familiarity with *its voice*, and learn *Jesus' voice* instead. As we'll see in a moment, the Bible, God's written word, becomes indispensable to us to retrain us and help us discern the new way from the old.

The Apostle John characterizes "the world," that is, the fallen state of man, in this way.

"[15] Do not love the world or anything in the world. If anyone loves the world, the love of the Father is not in him. [16] For everything in the world – the cravings of sinful man, the lust of his eyes and the boasting of what he has and does – comes

---

[57] "Constant use" (NIV), "by practice" (NRSV), "by constant practice" (ESV), "by reason of use" (KJV) is the noun *hexis*, "a habit, whether of body or of mind, a power acquired by custom, practice, use,"[57] which produces "a state of maturity" (BDAG 350).

not from the Father but from the world. [17] The world and its desires pass away, but the man who does the will of God lives forever." (1 John 2:15-17)

Ponder these verses and they'll help you understand what "the world's voice" might sound like. I really like J.B. Phillips' paraphrase of verse 16:

"The whole world-system, based as it is on men's primitive desires, their greedy ambitions and the glamour of all that they think splendid, is not derived from the Father at all, but from the world itself." (1 John 2:16)

There is a strong pull in us to conform to the values and standards of the culture around us. When we hear those voices, we need to recognize that this is not God's voice. His is distinctly different.

The Renewal of Our Minds (Romans 12:2)

As we'll see in a moment, the Scriptures are necessary to help us discern God's voice from the voices of the world, the flesh, and the devil. *Do not neglect daily reading of the Bible,* since it is necessary for the "renewing of your mind."

"Do not conform any longer to the pattern of this world, but be transformed by the renewing of your mind. Then you will be able to test and approve what God's will is – his good, pleasing and perfect will." (Romans 12:2)

The Bible has a cleansing power to those who are "washed" by reading it (Ephesians 5:26; John 17:17). It is designed to train us in what true righteousness is, so that we *can* discern. Paul writes:

"All Scripture is breathed out by God and profitable for teaching, for reproof, for correction, and for training in righteousness, that the man of God may be complete, equipped for every good work." (2 Timothy 3:16-17)

If you neglect Bible reading, it's likely that your mind won't be fully renewed, and you'll get yourself in deep trouble by straying off Jesus' Way, and not even be aware of it!

Q3. (Ephesians 2:1-3; 1 John 2:16). Give an example of what the voice of the flesh – our lusts and desires – might sound like. Give an example of what the voice of the world might sound like. Give an example of what the voice of the devil might sound like. Why is a knowledge of the Scripture necessary for discernment of these voices?

http://www.joyfulheart.com/forums/topic/1781-q3-discerning-voices/

Learn the Scriptures

One of our fears might be that we'll become like one of those whacko serial killers who "hears voices." Perhaps the most important way to discern what we think God is saying to us is to judge it by what God's word says.

I know that people can "prove" anything they want to by quoting some Scripture. But I also know that as we humbly read the Bible and seek to know God through his Word, we'll get a pretty good idea of the kind of behavior that conforms to God, and the behavior that goes against God. This is all about a relationship with your heavenly Father. As you read the Bible, you learn what pleases him.

For example, if you think God is telling you to go kill someone, I encourage you to talk to your pastor before carrying this out. Your pastor will explain (while taking you for a psych evaluation), that we are commanded not to murder (Exodus 20:13; Matthew 5:21; etc.)

If you feel God is telling you to divorce your wife and marry that beautiful young woman you are having an affair with, you can be sure it isn't God speaking to you, but rather the flesh and the devil! Paul writes:

> "The acts of the sinful nature are obvious: sexual immorality, impurity and debauchery; idolatry and witchcraft; hatred, discord, jealousy, fits of rage, selfish ambition, dissensions, factions and envy; drunkenness, orgies, and the like. I warn you, as I did before, that those who live like this will not inherit the kingdom of God. But the fruit of the Spirit is love, joy, peace, patience, kindness, goodness, faithfulness, gentleness and self-control. Against such things there is no law." (Galatians 5:19-23)

God is not going to tell you to do something that is contrary to what he says in his written Word! As you learn the Bible, you're able to discern the voices in your head.

There's a special bonus of regular reading of the Bible, however. Sometimes, God will "quicken" or make especially meaningful to you, a particular verse. This is a common way that God guides and speaks to us. It is wonderful to see the Holy Spirit shed brilliant light on a verse you had read 50 times before without really understanding!

Recognize and Surrender Your Desires

One of the strong voices in our head is our own desires, the voice of "the flesh." Desires aren't necessarily bad; they're a necessary part of what makes us humans. However, our desires are not necessarily aligned with God's desires.

Often, when we ask God about things, we have already developed our own personal preferences. It's a novice mistake to come to God with your pet project asking him to rubber stamp it for you with a "Yes." And that "Yes" is what we have preconditioned ourselves to hear.

Our problem is that we often have "selfish ambition"[58] (James 3:17) that can cloud or interfere with us hearing God's voice accurately. The key is to deliberately humble ourselves before God, rather than be quick to assume that God agrees with us.

I've found it extremely helpful when I'm asking God about situations or requesting things from him, to explicitly clarify my own personal desires before him in prayer. I sometimes make this kind of statement to God:

> "God what should I do about this situation? My own personal desire is to do such and such, but I really want what You want instead of what I want. So please help me get clarity on this. Show me what *You* want. Or if what You want is the same as what I want, please confirm that to me."

Of course, our example is Jesus in the Garden of Gethsemane.

> "'*Abba*, Father,' he said, 'everything is possible for you. Take this cup from me. Yet not what I will, but what you will.'" (Mark 14:36)

For us to be able to discern God's voice, we must be willing to obey once we determine what he is saying, as we discussed in Lesson 4. Without a willingness to obey, we may never know whether or not we are hearing God.

Acknowledge your own desires up front and fully surrender them. If you do so, you'll be able to better distinguish God's voice from your own desires.

Confess and Repent of any Known Sin

To be able to discern God's voice clearly, we can't be harboring or nursing sin. It is true God can speak to sinners. A number of examples come to mind, such as Sampson and Jonah. Rather than blessing rebellious sinners, however, God promises blessings to those who obey him. God is repulsed by those who sin at the same time they are offering sacrifices before God, pretending to be pious (Matthew 5:22-24).

---

[58] The Greek word *eritheia* in verse 14 is translated as "selfish ambition" (NIV, NRSV, ESV, NASB). Before New Testament times *eritheia* is found only rarely, "where it denotes a self-seeking pursuit of political office by unfair means…. "For Paul and his followers … the meaning 'strife, contentiousness' [KJV, as if the word were derived from *eris*, "strife, discord, contention"] cannot be excluded. But 'selfishness, selfish ambition' in all cases gives a sense that is just as good, and perhaps better" (BAGD 309).

Too often, sinners can't discern the still small voice, only the loud shout needed to break through a calloused heart. Unconfessed sin injures our relationship with God and a sin-calloused heart is less able to hear his whispers, detect his nudges, and respond. When we hold onto our sin, it distorts what we might hear from God, because when we hold onto our sins we are prone to justify them – even against God's clear Word.

For example, Peter warns husbands:

> "Husbands, in the same way be considerate as you live with your wives, and treat them with respect as the weaker partner and as heirs with you of the gracious gift of life, **so that nothing will hinder your prayers.**" (1 Peter 3:7)

However, don't wait until you're perfect to listen for God's voice – you'll be waiting a long time! We make mistakes. We sin. We sometimes sin grievously. But we must not linger there.

> "If we walk in the light, as he is in the light, we have fellowship with one another, and the blood of Jesus, his Son, purifies us from all sin. If we claim to be without sin, we deceive ourselves and the truth is not in us. If we confess our sins, he is faithful and just and will forgive us our sins and purify us from all unrighteousness." (1 John 1:7-9)

As you're listening to God and discerning, confess any known sins. Keep short accounts with God. This way you'll both (1) *want* to hear him, and (2) *be able to discern* his nudges and promptings.

> Q4. (Mark 14:36; 1 Peter 3:7) Why is it necessary to recognize and then surrender our desires when we are seeking God's will. What happens if we neglect to do this? How can holding on to sin distort what you think you are hearing from God? http://www.joyfulheart.com/forums/topic/1782-q4-not-my-will/

Inner Peace

In the context of being members of one body, Paul encourages peace.

> "Let the peace of Christ rule in your hearts,
> to which indeed you were called in one body;
> and be thankful" (Colossians 3:15).

"Peace" is used twice in the verse, as if to emphasize it. "Rule" is *brabeuō*, not the usual word for "rule." Originally it referred to the referee or umpire in the Greek games who would "award prizes in contests." Here it means by extension, "be in control of someone's activity by making a decision, be judge, decide, control, rule."[59]

In our lives, peace is to "call the shots." This can apply to keeping unity within the body, but I think inner peace also helps us as an inner barometer that God is leading us. In the same way a lack of inner peace might signal that we got something wrong and need to go back to God to recalibrate.

When we don't have peace about a direction that we thought was from God, this can be an indicator that we need to come to God again for clarification. Of course, this is subjective, and because of that, Satan can counterfeit lack of peace. So use this as one of several diagnostic tools to make sure you're getting God's direction clearly.

Don't Be Rushed

In my experience, God's voice is gentle but firm. Satan's voice, on the other hand, can often be pushy, compulsive, in a hurry, demanding, nagging like someone you'd like to shut up. Satan's voice is often condemning, sarcastic, accusing, shaming, etc. As you begin to hear God's voice and promptings, you'll start to recognize his gentle voice. Don't be pushed to do something "right now!" God generally guides us with enough time to evaluate.

Having said that, when God speaks to us or nudges us, we shouldn't spend a lot of time deciding whether or not to obey. Some of God's nudges are time sensitive. If we don't act soon, it'll be too late.

For example, I can remember as a college junior being in downtown Los Angeles, returning to catch a bus back to college, when God prompted me to turn right on the next street – not the way to the bus stop. I turned right, and had a wonderful adventure of seeing God work in a man's life. Sometimes God will nudge us to begin a conversation with a stranger – or with someone we know. If we wait too long, we miss the opportunity.

Now let's step back while I qualify my previous statement about Satan's voice sometimes being demanding. I'm speaking in general terms. However, Satan *can* disguise himself as an angel of light to deceive you (2 Corinthians 11:14), so be wise! This could terrify

---

[59] *Brabeuō*, BDAG 183.

us if we were spiritual babies. But as we trust the Lord and grow in Christ, we venture out without fear because "we are not ignorant of his schemes"[60] (2 Corinthians 2:11).

In the same way, God's voice is gentle, even if he rebukes us at times. I don't remember anger in any of God's promptings to me, but sometimes disappointment.

I don't have a scriptural hook to hang all this on. I share these subjective, touchy-feely impressions from my personal experience of God's voice. If this doesn't make sense to you, that's okay.

Counsel with a Spiritual Brother or Sister

Being part of a healthy Christian community has a great many benefits. One of these is being able to talk to your pastor or to spiritual men or women in your congregation, to make sure you're on the right track. So find a spiritually mature person who seeks God, someone you feel you can trust, who might serve as a mentor.

"Where there is no guidance, a people falls,
but in an abundance of counselors there is safety." (Proverbs 11:14, ESV)

When I was in college in Los Angeles, I had an opportunity to go to a conference in Texas, where churches in my fellowship would gather annually for worship and sharing. I prayed about it, but received no guidance. I hoped that someone would prophesy over me, "Go, thou, to the conference," but no one did. So I asked a mature brother. I'll never forget his counsel. He said something like, "The guidance system on a missile doesn't really begin guiding it until it lifts off the ground. Do what you think God is leading you to do and trust him to correct you if you're on the wrong path." That helped! I went to the conference and God dealt with me in several important ways. I knew later from the results in my life that God wanted me there.

Having said that, don't do something just because someone you trust tells you to. But seriously consider their advice before the Lord, as one of the ways he confirms his will to you.

> Q5. (Proverbs 11:14) Why is it valuable to counsel with spiritual people in the Christian community when we're learning to discern God's voice? How is having a spiritual mentor helpful? What is the danger of always going to another person to

---

[60] "Scheme" (NIV), "design" (NRSV), "device" (KJV) is *noēma*, "that which one has in mind as product of intellectual process," here "design, purpose, intention," from *noeō*, "to perceive with the mind, think upon, ponder" (BDAG 675, 1b; Thayer 426).

confirm God's word? Why is out-growing a mentor a common occurrence? http://www.joyfulheart.com/forums/topic/1783-q5-counselors-and-mentors/

The Voice of the Spirit (John 10:3-5; Romans 8:16; 1 John 2:20, 27)

Jesus promises us in the Parable of the Good Shepherd that we'll be able to "know his voice".

> "3 The watchman opens the gate for him, and the sheep listen[61] to his voice. He calls[62] his own sheep by name[63] and leads them out. 4 When he has brought out all his own, he goes on ahead of them, and his sheep follow him because they know his voice. 5 But they will never follow a stranger; in fact, they will run away from him because they do not recognize a stranger's voice." (John 10:3-5)

Jesus and the Father sent the Holy Spirit to function as our internal teacher, as we learn to become sensitive to Him. John Wesley referred to this as the inner "witness of the Spirit" (Romans 8:16). The Apostle John speaks of the continuing teaching presence of the Spirit as "an anointing from the Holy One" (1 John 2:20), and "his anointing [that] teaches you about all things" (1 John 2:27).

As we walk with Jesus, we become attuned to his voice, the voice of the Spirit.

You Can Trust Your Shepherd

Don't be afraid of questioning what you think you are hearing from God. Your questioning and seeking to discern doesn't mean that you are an unbeliever, but rather that you care to hear God accurately. In a similar way, congregations are encouraged to test prophecy and evaluate it, only accepting that which seems like it is from God (1 Thessalonians 5:23; 1 Corinthians 14:29).

Just like children learning to walk, or obey, or anything else, loving parents understand where the children are in their growth and make allowances for them. Your heavenly Father loves you. He is fully able to teach you. So long as your heart sincerely seeks him, he

---

[61] "Listen" (NIV), "hear" (NRSV, KJV) is *akouō*, "hear," but here with the idea of "to give careful attention to, listen to, heed someone"(BDAG 38, 4).

[62] "Calls" is *phōneō*, "to produce a voiced sound/tone, frequently with reference to intensity of tone," here, "to call to oneself, summon" (BDAG 107, 3).

[63] "By name" (*kat' onoma*).

is pleased, even if you might fall down while learning to walk. Even if you make a mistake. You can trust him always, for he loves you!

Lessons for Disciples

We've discussed a number of guidelines to help us discern God's voice from the other voices vying for our attention.

1. Asking God for confirmation, like Gideon. When we really desire to know his will and aren't yet sure of his voice, seeking confirmation pleases our Father (Judges 6:36-38).

2. "Putting God to the test" springs from a heart of unbelief (and perhaps rebellion), that demands that God fulfill some sign before we believe in him. This is a heart difference, a motivational difference from asking God for confirmation.

3. Our task is to discern God's true voice and promptings from the other voices in our head: the world, the flesh, the devil, and our conscience.

4. We can't learn to discern God's voice without making mistakes; this is a learning process. However, we can learn to discern.

5. We've been used to listening to the voice of the world and the devil. God's word helps us recognize the difference between their voices and God's way (Ephesians 2:1-3; 1 John 2:15-17).

6. When we explicitly recognize and then surrender our own ambitions and desires to God in prayer, we are better able to distinguish between them and God's will, as did Jesus in the Garden of Gethsemane (Mark 14:36).

7. Getting to know the Scriptures by daily reading helps us discern God's voice from other voices, to distinguish the acts of the flesh from the fruit of the Spirit (Galatians 5:19-23), by the renewing of our minds (Romans 12:2). If we neglect daily Bible reading, we can get in deep trouble without hardly being aware it.

8. One bonus of reading the Bible is that the Holy Spirit sometimes "quickens" or makes certain verses alive to us that we've passed over before.

9. To discern God's voice clearly, we must confess and repent of any known sin, which injures our relationship with God and makes our heart calloused, that is, less able to hear God's whispers and nudges, and respond to them (1 Peter 3:7; 1 John 1:7-9).

10. The presence or absence of "inner peace" is another way to discern God's leading (Colossians 3:15).

11. God's voice is gentle but firm; Satan's voice, on the other hand can sometimes be compulsive and pushy. Nevertheless, realize that Satan can disguise himself as an angel of light, so be wise.

12. Being part of a Christian community provides safety to us, since we can find spiritual men and women who can counsel us and help us discern God's voice (Proverbs 11:14).

13. The Holy Spirit provides an inner witness of our relationship to the Good Shepherd. "My sheep listen to my voice; I know them, and they follow me" (John 10:27). The Paraclete, the Holy Spirit also teaches us and leads us into all truth (John 14-16; 1 John 2:20, 27).

14. It's not wrong to seek to discern what you believe God is showing you, just as it is not wrong to test prophecy to make sure it is from God (1 Thessalonians 5:23; 1 Corinthians 14:29).

15. As you're learning all this, you can trust your Father, who understands that it takes children some time – and some falls – to learn to walk. God loves you!

Week 5 Assignment. Converse with God While Around Other People

So far you might assume that you can only hear God if there is stillness around you. Not so. Once you've begun to discern his voice in the quietness, you'll begin to recognize his voice when lots is going on around you.

As your communication system gets better established, God can use you as his agent any place, any time. That's where all this is going – to be God's servants, disciples ready and willing to do the Master's bidding 24/7.

So your assignment this week is to talk to him during your day, especially when you're around other people. Pray quick prayers – "God, bless Helen over there. She seems like she is having a hard day." You may find that God nudges you to engage Helen in a conversation and encourage her – perhaps pray for her. Then share this with your mentor and spiritual partner. Even if you *thought* you should have engaged Helen, but were afraid to do so, share that. This is all a process of discerning God's voice and promptings, and then being willing to obey without questioning.

This is the last weekly assignment, but I encourage you to continue your conversations with your mentor and spiritual partner, so you can continue to learn and establish as a way of life, listening for God's voice and then obeying him.

Wrapping It Up

That's about it. Here's the journey we've been on.

1. **Listening as a Biblical Pattern (Mark 1:35; John 5:19).** In Lesson 1 we examined examples of Jesus' own dependence upon the Father, how he ministered in the power of the Spirit, how he promises that the Holy Spirit will come to us and help us (John 14-16). We also studied how the Spirit reveals to us the mind of Christ (1 Corinthians 2:9-16).

2. **Recognizing God's Voice (1 Kings 19).** In Lesson 2 we explored how God speaks in words and sentences to guide and encourage his servants. We examined Elijah's "still small voice," plus words of encouragement to Paul and others.

3. **Nudges and No (Acts 8:26-40; 16:6-10).** In Lesson 3 we discussed how many times God's voice is heard more in promptings or "no," rather than in articulate sentences. We examined Philip and the Ethiopian eunuch (Acts 8:26-40), and how the apostles were seeking where to preach (and where not to preach) on Paul's Second Missionary Journey (Acts 16:6-10). We saw the yeses and noes of David inquiring of the Lord, and discussed God's promptings as perhaps a kind of "word of knowledge" for ministry to people, alongside other everyday nudges.

4. **Heart Preparation for Listening to God (1 Samuel 3:1-10).** In Lesson 4 we explored heart preparation for listening for God, beginning with the boy Samuel (1 Samuel 3:1-10), who prayed, "Speak, Lord, for your servant is listening." We saw an emphasis on a willingness to be a "servant," to be willing to obey and follow instructions. We also examined the subtle dangers of pride, and the centrality of earnestly seeking an intimate relationship with God, rather than desiring the mere "novelty" of hearing God's voice.

5. **Discerning God's Voice (Judges 6:36-40).** Finally, in Lesson 5 we studied Gideon's putting a fleece before the Lord. We examined ways to discern whether it is God speaking, rather than one of the other voices in our heads. We also talked about the safety of working with a spiritual partner or mentor within the Christian community, knowing the Scriptures, and clarifying and surrendering our own desires as we ask God for his guidance.

There are many more stories in the Bible of men and women hearing from God. But we've looked at the basic principles. I hope that you've been doing the weekly exercises. If so, you're well on your way to listening for God's voice.

If you haven't been taking steps to put into practice what you've been learning, you're in serious spiritual danger. Is this just an intellectual exercise for you? Are you just a "hearer" of the word, but not a "doer," thus deceiving yourself? (James 1:22). I urge you, in Jesus' name, to diligently seek to know Jesus and to listen for his voice so that you may be a faithful and productive Jesus-disciple today!

Okay, friends. We've spent time together learning how to listen for and discern God's voice. Now it's up to you. Go out there and "give them heaven"!

Prayer

Father, thank you that your Spirit will guide us into all truth. Please help us as we seek to recognize your voice. Help us be willing to venture – and to fail – as we learn to follow you, trusting you always that "you have our back," that you seek our best. We love you. Help us to listen for, hear, and then obey you when you speak to us. In Jesus' name, we pray. Amen.

Key Verses

"Gideon said to God, 'If you will save Israel by my hand as you have promised – look, I will place a wool fleece on the threshing floor. If there is dew only on the fleece and all the ground is dry, then I will know that you will save Israel by my hand, as you said.' And that is what happened. Gideon rose early the next day; he squeezed the fleece and wrung out the dew – a bowlful of water." Then Gideon said to God, 'Do not be angry with me. Let me make just one more request. Allow me one more test with the fleece. This time make the fleece dry and the ground covered with dew.' That night God did so. Only the fleece was dry; all the ground was covered with dew." (Judges 6:36-40, NIV)

"Do not **test** the LORD your God as you did at Massah." (Deuteronomy 6:16, NIV)

"It is also written: 'Do not put the Lord your God to the **test.**'" (Matthew 4:7, NIV)

"For Jews demand signs and Greeks seek wisdom…." (1 Corinthians 1:22, NIV)

"But solid food is for the mature, who by constant use have trained themselves to distinguish good from evil." (Hebrews 5:14, NIV)

"The watchman opens the gate for him, and the sheep listen to his voice. He calls his own sheep by name and leads them out. When he has brought out all his own, he goes on ahead of them, and his sheep follow him because they know his voice.

But they will never follow a stranger; in fact, they will run away from him because they do not recognize a stranger's voice." (John 10:3-5, NIV)

"As for you, you were dead in your transgressions and sins, in which you used to live when you followed the ways of this world and of the ruler of the kingdom of the air, the spirit who is now at work in those who are disobedient. All of us also lived among them at one time, gratifying the cravings of our sinful nature and following its desires and thoughts. Like the rest, we were by nature objects of wrath." (Ephesians 2:1-3, NIV)

"Do not love the world or anything in the world. If anyone loves the world, the love of the Father is not in him. For everything in the world – the cravings of sinful man, the lust of his eyes and the boasting of what he has and does – comes not from the Father but from the world. The world and its desires pass away, but the man who does the will of God lives forever." (1 John 2:15-17, NIV)

"'*Abba*, Father,' he said, 'everything is possible for you. Take this cup from me. Yet not what I will, but what you will.'" (Mark 14:36, NIV)

"The acts of the sinful nature are obvious: sexual immorality, impurity and debauchery; idolatry and witchcraft; hatred, discord, jealousy, fits of rage, selfish ambition, dissensions, factions and envy; drunkenness, orgies, and the like. I warn you, as I did before, that those who live like this will not inherit the kingdom of God. But the fruit of the Spirit is love, joy, peace, patience, kindness, goodness, faithfulness, gentleness and self-control. Against such things there is no law." (Galatians 5:19-23, NIV)

"Do not conform any longer to the pattern of this world, but be transformed by the renewing of your mind. Then you will be able to test and approve what God's will is – his good, pleasing and perfect will." (Romans 12:2, NIV)

"Husbands, in the same way be considerate as you live with your wives, and treat them with respect as the weaker partner and as heirs with you of the gracious gift of life, so that nothing will hinder your prayers." (1 Peter 3:7, NIV)

"If we walk in the light, as he is in the light, we have fellowship with one another, and the blood of Jesus, his Son, purifies us from all sin. If we claim to be without sin, we deceive ourselves and the truth is not in us. If we confess our sins, he is faithful and just and will forgive us our sins and purify us from all unrighteousness." (1 John 1:7-9, NIV)

"Let the peace of Christ rule in your hearts, to which indeed you were called in one body; and be thankful" (Colossians 3:15, NIV).

"Where there is no guidance, a people falls,
but in an abundance of counselors there is safety." (Proverbs 11:14, ESV)

Appendix 1. Participant Handouts

If you are working with a class or small group, feel free to duplicate the following handouts at no additional charge. If you'd like to print 8-1/2" x 11" or A4 size pages, you can download the free Participant Guide handout sheets at:

www.jesuswalk.com/voice/voice-lesson-handouts.pdf

Discussion Questions

You'll typically find 4 or 5 questions for each lesson. Each question may include several sub-questions. These are designed to get group members engaged in discussion of the key points of the passage. If you're running short of time, feel free to skip questions or portions of questions.

Suggestions for Classes and Groups

Individuals who are studying online can probably complete one full lesson per week, though they'll need to be diligent to do so. But some of the chapters just have too much material for a one hour class discussion. Feel free to arrange the lessons any way that works best for your group.

Because of the length of these handouts – and to keep down the page count so we can keep the book price lower – they are being made available at no cost online.

www.jesuswalk.com/voice/voice-lesson-handouts.pdf

Appendix 2. Assignments to Sensitize You to God's Voice

Since we're trying to develop a skill of listening for God's voice, each lesson includes a practical assignment for you to put into practice in your life that week. This is not an academic study of Bible theory, but a practical study that will result in your life being changed.

Week 0 Assignment. Get Ready. Find a Mentor, a Spiritual Partner, and a Notebook

(To be completed before you begin the first lesson)

As you begin this series of lessons to help you discern God's voice, I want you to find a mentor – or at least a peer with whom you can share in this new lifestyle.

Edward Burne-Jones, 'Eli with Samuel' (1897), stained glass, Martin's Church, Brampton, Cumbria, England. The design was first used at Christ's Church, Oxford (1872).

Listening for God's voice and promptings, and then doing what he shows you to do, is a learned skill of sorts. But it is more than that, it is an exciting way of life.

Manual skills can be learned by watching YouTube videos. But how does a new police officer become sensitized to the problems and crimes of a neighborhood? By riding along with a more experienced officer who points things out that the average person just doesn't see. In the process, the novice officer acquires trained eyes.

Though God has helped many people learn to hear and identify God's voice and promptings on their own, that is not the easiest way to learn. It is best to **find a mentor** in your church or community to whom you can go with questions that may come up. *Make sure this is someone who actually believes in and practices listening for God.* In some churches your pastor might be this person. Or it might be a spiritually mature man or woman. On some occasions, your mentor might even attend a different church. Nevertheless, diligently search out this person by prayer and by suggestions of others.

In addition to a mentor, you need to **find a spiritual partner** who can walk this journey with you. You'll learn from each other and be able to bounce ideas off of each other. When I was in college, Edson Lee was my dormmate. We went to the same church on Sunday. But during the week we learned together a great deal together about listening to and obeying God. I can remember at the end of a day, we'd get together to share about how we had seen God in action that day. One of us would always say, "God sure knows what he is doing!"

Note: In this course we share responses to discussion questions in an online forum. But I think it is best to share your experiences in hearing God's voice with your spiritual partner and mentor, who know you, *not* online. The reason is this. In any kind of cyber sharing, people can't know you in your real-life context. Helpful, honest feedback on hearing God's voice needs to take that context into consideration. For our spiritual partners we need people who can get to know us in a more rounded way than someone would be able to online.

So find a mentor if you can – and for sure find a spiritual partner, a peer who is willing to walk this portion of the journey with you. Get this person to sign up for this study with you. Then get together often, in person or on the phone, to share how you see God working.

Beyond a mentor and a spiritual partner, **you'll need a notebook or journal** in which to write down what God is showing you. It's best if your notebook has decent binding so the pages don't start falling out. I found a journal a similar size to my Bible. What I settled on was a brand called Markings, a 5" x 8" journal by C.R. Gibson (markings.com), widely available in the United States. But really, any notebook will do. Make it a point to get one for this study.

It's absolutely essential for you to **begin or renew a daily Quiet Time**, 5 to 10 minutes (or more) that you spend with God in prayer, reading Scripture, and listening. I'll talk more about that in Lesson 1, but start today!

Week 1 Assignment. Set Aside a Regular Quiet Time to Spend with God

As a way of patterning yourself after Jesus, who sought the Father early and often, set aside for yourself a regular Quiet Time to spend with God. You may be already doing this. If so, great. But even if you already do this, it's time to "up your game," to renew this time so it is most meaningful.

Set aside at least five to ten minutes a day – or more, depending on your schedule – preferably in the morning when you have your whole day ahead of you.

Your Quiet Time is a time to touch base with your Friend and renew your relationship with him each day. It is also a discipline that serious Christians set up in their lives – whether they feel like it or not. Sometimes you'll be sluggish and not very spiritually in tune. Have your Quiet Time anyway; that's when you need it the most. Sometimes your Quiet Time may seem like just going through the motions. Do it anyway. Sometimes God meets you wonderfully in your Quiet Time. Rejoice!

Here's a simple guideline for a Quiet Time.[64]

1. **Greeting**. "Good morning, Father," is the way I often begin.
2. **Praise**. The Psalmist encourages us: "Worship the LORD with gladness; come into his presence with singing (Psalm 100:2; NRSV). Offer verbal praise: "Lord, I come before you with thanksgiving and praise this morning." Perhaps sing a praise chorus.
3. **Scripture**. Ask God to open his Word to you. Then read a portion of Scripture, not just a verse from a devotional guide. But read systematically. You might begin with the Gospel of Mark or the Gospel of John and read a chapter a day. Each day, pick up from where you left off the day before. I try to read a chapter from the Old Testament, a Psalm, and a chapter from the New Testament each day. There's no right or wrong way here. However, whatever your practice is, stick with it – and don't coddle yourself! Over time, this regularity makes you acquainted with the whole Word of God. This helps you know the lines along which God is thinking, his values, and what pleases him. Then as God begins to speak or prompt you, you'll be able to discern whether it is God or not.
4. **Prayer**. There's an acronym ACTS – Adoration, Confession, Thanksgiving, Supplication – that is a useful guide. I confess my sins to God, and ask him to cleanse me (1 John 1:9). Then I bring before the Lord each of the people close to me and ask God to help them. Sometimes as I'm praying for someone, God will prompt me with some way I can minister to him or her.
5. **Listening.** We'll amplify this step in Lesson 2.
6. **Take notes.** Some people call this "journaling." It doesn't have to be formal, but be prepared to write down what God seems to be showing you.

Sometimes my pattern for my Quiet Time seems to grow stale. Then I mix it up, perhaps reading a devotional book along with scripture and prayer. Perhaps spending more

---

[64] For more see my article, "Apply Fertilizer Liberally." www.joyfulheart.com/maturity/fertil.htm

time singing. At least for a while. Then I usually return to my usual pattern after a few weeks.

Over the years I've observed that people who have a regular Quiet Time are the ones who grow as disciples. Greg Krieger sees spiritual disciplines such as a Quiet Time as a way of putting up all the sails to catch the slightest breeze of the Spirit's whisperings.

Setting up a daily Quiet Time is your assignment for this week. Then talk to your spiritual partner and explain what your plan is. Later in the week, share how this is going. It's easier to form new habits when you have some accountability built in.

Week 2 Assignment. Learn to Quiet Yourself and Listen

One of the chief reasons we miss God's voice is because we don't take time to listen. We rush through our devotions and then we're off to work or making breakfast or dinner, or something. We don't take time to listen.

I've found that it's much easier to quiet myself at the *beginning* of the day, before I review my e-mail and read the news. Those activities get my mind going a mile-a-minute in all sorts of directions. So the best time to spend with God is before I begin the activities of the day, when the day is new and my spirit is fresh.

I understand that this doesn't work for everyone. If you're a new mother, for example, there may not be quiet at the beginning of the day. Or you may not be a "morning person." You'll need to find some work-arounds, different times of the day when you can take some minutes with God by yourself.

If there are people around, explain that you're going to be praying for a few minutes. Then withdraw into your own thoughts. The more you do this, the better you'll be at it.

Whatever time and place works best in your circumstances, know that one of the keys to hearing God is to quiet yourself before him. The Quakers call it "centering down," quieting one's mind and spirit before God. My pastor sings simple, repetitive praise songs. Some traditions repeat a prayer over and over again. Others recommend breathing in and out, listening to your breathing as a way of quieting your thoughts.

I usually focus my attention on God through praise and worship. I might sing a hymn or praise chorus, or read a psalm. I've found that when I read silently, my mind can wander to other things. But when I read aloud it's easier to keep focus. I find that as I spend a few minutes in worship, my thoughts become less scattered and become aligned with God's.

These are all techniques to quiet one's spirit. Don't get hung up on the virtues of one technique over another. Your purpose here is to get the swirling currents of your mind quieted all flowing in the same direction – towards God.

Once your spirit has become quiet, I encourage you to talk to God about what's going on in your life and listen.

"Be still, and know that I am God." (Psalm 46:10)

"The LORD is in his holy temple;
let all the earth be silent before him." (Habakkuk 2:20)

Your assignment this week is to practice quieting your spirit before the Lord so you can listen. Then talk to your mentor and/or spiritual partner about your experiences of quieting your spirit before God.

Week 3 Assignment. Sensitize Yourself: Where Have You Seen God Lately?

At Rock Harbor Covenant Church where I attend, a common question we're encouraged to ask one another is, "Where have you seen God lately?"

It's sometimes an embarrassing question. Long silences ensue. But the purpose of the question is to train us to recognize God at work around us – in the little things as well as the occasional big things.

God is constantly at work. He doesn't stop for rest days (John 5:17). Our problem is that our eyes aren't trained to see him at work. What we see, we attribute exclusively to human causation. If we're to discern God's voice, this has to change. We have to become sensitive to him working all around us. Jesus said,

"I tell you the truth, the Son can do nothing by himself; he can do only what he sees his Father doing, because whatever the Father does the Son also does." (John 5:19)

Learning to discern God at work is foundational to training yourself to hear his voice and pick up on his whispers, promptings, and nudges. Your assignment this week is to talk with your spiritual partner every day, and ask the question, "Where have you seen God working today?" Then explain where you have seen God at work that day.

Week 4 Assignment. Ask God Questions and Listen for His Response

You may have started doing this already, but if not, after you have quieted your spirit before him, begin to ask God questions about what's going on in your life. Then be silent and listen to see what God might say to you.

You may receive some distinct impressions, thoughts he may put in your mind – or not. When you feel God is saying something to you, write it down in your journal. Just the act of writing down what you think God might be saying will help clarify it for you. Then ask him about what you think you're hearing. Perhaps you'll hear more. This is a conversation.

You won't always hear God say something. That's okay. Don't try to force God to speak to you or to answer you! He is the sovereign God, not you. Content yourself to be humbly silent in his presence where you can find your spirit renewed.

Nevertheless, you may find him putting thoughts in your mind. If so, praise God. That's a good start.

Your assignment this week is – every day in your Quiet Time – to ask God questions and then be still and listen. If he puts something in your mind write it down. Then share this with your spiritual partner, who may be able to help you discern if this is, indeed, God. Eventually you'll learn to discern God's voice on your own. But in the beginning, feedback from a sympathetic friend is helpful and encouraging.

Week 5 Assignment. Converse with God While Around Other People

So far you might assume that you can only hear God if there is stillness around you. Not so. Once you've begun to discern his voice in the quietness, you'll begin to recognize his voice when lots is going on around you.

As your communication system gets better established, God can use you as his agent any place, any time. That's where all this is going – to be God's servants, disciples ready and willing to do the Master's bidding 24/7.

So your assignment this week is to talk to him during your day, especially when you're around other people. Pray quick prayers – "God, bless Helen over there. She seems like she is having a hard day." You may find that God nudges you to engage Helen in a conversation and encourage her – perhaps pray for her. Then share this with your mentor and spiritual partner. Even if you *thought* you should have engaged Helen, but were afraid to do so, share that. This is all a process of discerning God's voice and promptings, and then being willing to obey without questioning.

This is the last weekly assignment, but I encourage you to continue your conversations with your mentor and spiritual partner, so you can continue to learn and establish as a way of life, listening for God's voice and then obeying him.

Appendix 3. Bibliography

There have been many books written on this subject over the years. These are brief notes on some I'm familiar with.

Blackaby, Henry and Richard, *Hearing God's Voice* (B&H Publishing, 2002). Among other things, a practical guide to how to discern God's voice from others. Well done.

Deere, Jack, *Surprised by the Voice of God* (Zondervan, 1996). Written by former Dallas Theological Seminary professor who learned that God does actually speak today. In this excellent work, he carefully develops the texts in the Bible, against "cessationists" who tend to be uncomfortable with the voice of God in our day as a threat to the sufficiency of Scripture.

Eldredge, John, *Walking with God: Talk to Him. Hear from Him. Really* (Thomas Nelson, 2008). A personal narrative day by day of how it works to listen and walk with God. Not a comprehensive look, but an example of how it might work.

Jacobs, Cindy, *The Voice of God: How God Speaks Personally and Corporately to His Children Today* (Regal, 1995), forward by Jack Hayford. This book is primarily on the gifts of prophecy and the word of knowledge, not specifically on an individual hearing God's voice for oneself and one's own ministry.

Willard, Dallas, *Hearing God: Developing a Conversational Relationship with God* (InterVarsity, 1984, 1989, 1999), previously published under the title, *In Search of Guidance*. An excellent treatment by a USC professor of philosophy who defines, asks hard questions, and points to Scripture and his own experience, and that of others.

CPSIA information can be obtained
at www.ICGtesting.com
Printed in the USA
BVHW062141180522
637342BV00005B/121